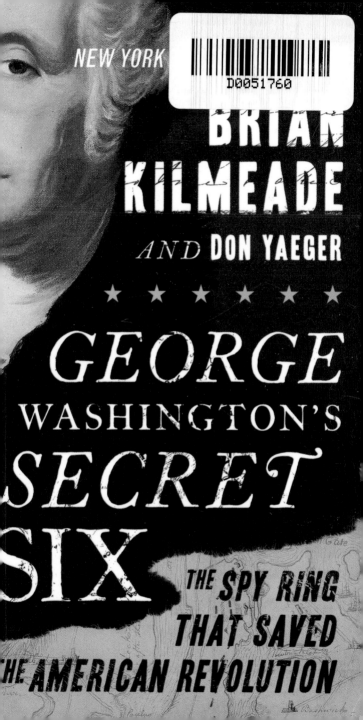

NEW YORK

D0051760

BRIAN KILMEADE

AND DON YAEGER

★ ★ ★ ★ ★ ★ ★

GEORGE
WASHINGTON'S
SECRET
SIX

THE SPY RING
THAT SAVED
THE AMERICAN REVOLUTION

SENTINEL

| U.S. | **$9.99** |
| CAN. | $13.50 |

Praise for *George Washington's Secret Six*

"Freedom is not free, never has been, and never will be. Kilmeade and Yaeger have done a wonderful job in reminding us all of the cost. Great read."
> —General Tommy Franks (U.S. Army, retired)

"Fast paced, factual, entertaining . . . and important!"
> —Michael Hayden, former director of the National Security Agency and the Central Intelligence Agency

"A historical gem. I loved it." —Donald Trump

"We would not have won the Revolution and secured our freedom were it not for the leadership of George Washington and the courage of the spies he set in motion. *George Washington's Secret Six* is a gripping and informative read."
> —Congressman Pete King, chairman of the Counterterrorism and Intelligence Subcommittee, House of Representatives Committee on Homeland Security

"A rollicking read by Kilmeade and Yaeger, acknowledging a long-overdue debt to six American heroes."
> —Karl Rove

"It would have been an honor to have served with Robert Townsend and the rest of the Culper spies in any of the deep-cover intelligence operations I spearheaded over twenty-seven years."
> —Wayne Simmons, coauthor of *The Natanz Directive*; CIA–Outside Paramilitary Special Operations

"The greatest true spy story in American history. . . . The spies . . . seem to have stepped from the pages of Robert Ludlum rather than a history book. . . . Anyone who wants to know how a handful of dedicated American patriots managed to defeat the greatest empire on earth needs to read this book."

—Arthur Herman, Pulitzer Prize finalist; author of the *New York Times* bestseller *How the Scots Invented the Modern World* and *Freedom's Forge: How American Business Produced Victory in World War II*

"A fast paced, meticulously researched espionage thriller . . . This is not your daddy's history class. This is more likely the precursor of a Hollywood blockbuster with spies, sex, betrayal, and murder all unfolding in a true story important to understanding how the American Revolution was won. Why couldn't my high school teachers have taught this one?"

—Doug Wead, historian and *New York Times* bestselling author

"*George Washington's Secret Six* is about patriots, by patriots, and for patriots. A compelling story of unsung heroes and war in the shadows during our Revolution, this superbly done book is as much a pleasure to read as it is illuminating (to include a fine, very human portrayal of Washington). Very strongly recommended as a gift for those who love history—and for Americans of all ages who need to learn more about our nation's past and the amazing courage that paid for our country's freedom."

—Ralph Peters, author of *Cain at Gettysburg* and *Hell or Richmond*

"James Bond is a rank amateur compared to the heroic efforts of the Culper Ring. Brian Kilmeade and Don Yaeger's work demonstrates why the story of the 'Secret Six' should be anything but a secret in American history."

—Harvey Mackay, author of *Swim with the Sharks Without Being Eaten Alive*

SENTINEL

GEORGE WASHINGTON'S SECRET SIX

Brian Kilmeade cohosts Fox News Channel's morning show *Fox & Friends* and also hosts the nationally syndicated radio show *Kilmeade & Friends*. He is the author of five books, and he lives on Long Island.

Don Yaeger has written or cowritten twenty-four books, including eight *New York Times* bestsellers. He lives in Tallahassee, Florida.

They are the coauthors of the *New York Times* bestseller *Thomas Jefferson and the Tripoli Pirates*.

BRIAN KILMEADE
AND DON YAEGER

GEORGE WASHINGTON'S *SECRET* SIX

THE SPY RING THAT SAVED THE AMERICAN REVOLUTION

SENTINEL

SENTINEL

An imprint of Penguin Random House LLC
375 Hudson Street
New York, New York 10014
penguin.com

First published in the United States of America by Sentinel,
a member of Penguin Group (USA) LLC, 2013
Published with a new afterword in 2014
This edition published 2016

Illustration credits
Collection of the New-York Historical Society: Insert page 2, bottom: no. 1940.16;
page 6, top: no. 87315d; page 6, bottom: no. 45397; page 7, top: no. 87312d;
page 7, bottom: no. 87311d.
Credits for other illustrations appear adjacent to the respective images.

THE LIBRARY OF CONGRESS HAS CATALOGED THE HARDCOVER EDITION AS FOLLOWS:
Kilmeade, Brian.
George Washington's secret six: the spy ring that saved the American
Revolution / Brian Kilmeade and Don Yaeger.
pages cm
Includes bibliographical references and index.
ISBN 978-1-59523-103-1 (hc.)
ISBN 978-1-59523-110-9 (pbk.)
ISBN 978-0-14-313060-4 (mass market pbk.)
1. United States—History—Revolution, 1775–1783—Secret service.
2. New York (State)—History—Revolution, 1775–1783—Secret service.
3. Spies—United States—History—18th century.
4. Spies—New York (State)—History—18th century.
5. Washington, George, 1732–1799—Friends and associates.
6. Townsend, Robert, 1753–1838.   I. Yaeger, Don.   II. Title.
E279.K55 2013
973.4'1092—dc23
2013032285

Printed in the United States of America
1   3   5   7   9   10   8   6   4   2

Set in Bulmer MT Std
Designed by Spring Hoteling

This book is dedicated to my Fantastic Five—wife, Dawn; son, Bryan; daughters, Kirstyn and Kaitlyn; and my incredible mom—who have heard me talk about this story for years, spent countless hours researching it, and urged me to write this book. Finally, it's done.

—B.K.

Tiffany: You are a pro's pro, one of the best writers I've ever worked with. I'm honored you're on my team.

—D.Y.

Washington did not really outfight
the British, he simply outspied us!

MAJOR GEORGE BECKWITH,
BRITISH INTELLIGENCE OFFICER 1782–1783

CONTENTS

Contents

AUTHORS' NOTE

Much of the dialogue contained in this book is fictional, but it is based on conversations that did take place and, wherever possible, incorporates actual phrases used by the speaker.

PREFACE

How do you discover the identity of a spy—someone whose main concern is remaining anonymous—who has been dead for nearly a century? That was the mission of Morton Pennypacker, Long Island's premier historian, during the 1920s. He knew the Americans would not have won the Revolutionary War without the Culper Spy Ring, but he didn't know the identity of the ring's most valuable member.

The spies' contributions included uncovering a British counterfeiting scheme, preventing an ambush of French reinforcements, smuggling a British naval codebook to Yorktown, and (most important) preventing Benedict Arnold from carrying out one of the greatest acts of treachery in American history: his plan to surrender West Point to the enemy.

Although these events were recorded as part of Revolutionary War history, none of them were attributed to any individual or group. No plaques attested to the brave work of the men and women responsible for alerting George Washington to the plots; no statues were erected in their honor. The six members of the Culper Spy Ring had served Washington under one condition: their names and activities were never to be revealed. Washington kept his promise, but he also kept their letters.

By the 1920s, the passing years had revealed the identities of most of the spies, but two—including that of the ring's chief spy—were still in question. Pennypacker, a relentless, solemn archivist, made it his personal mission to identify the principal spy, the unknown man who fed George Washington crucial information about the British presence in New York City and helped turn the tide of the Revolutionary War. He needed a name to finally solve the mystery of the man Washington had lauded in his letters but never met. Pennypacker believed that if he could give a name to the man known only by the pseudonym "Culper Junior," then this citizen-spy and all those who served in the ring with him could ascend to their rightful, prominent place alongside Paul Revere, Patrick Henry, Betsy Ross, and the rest of America's most famous Patriots.

Pennypacker was no stranger to intricate historical detective work, but for years his efforts brought him no closer to solving the mystery. And then a phone call in the summer of 1929 changed everything.

Whenever the telephone rang at Morton Pennypacker's house, the call was almost always about the history of New York, not a social event—and this particular call was no exception.

"We've found some Townsend family papers," a voice crackled on the other end of the line. "Do you have any interest in sifting through them?"

A few days later, the yellowed sheets of paper were piled high on his desk. Pennypacker handled each one gingerly, as if it were made of spun gold. Anything with the name Townsend dating to the eighteenth century was considered historically significant by Long Island historians. The Townsend family had been on American soil since the sixteen hundreds, and a prominent family in Oyster Bay, Long Island, since before the Revolution. Any scraps of ledgers or old bills would help create a more complete picture of the family's history, and Pennypacker was eager to see what new details he might learn.

Townsend papers were fairly ordinary finds, but something about these particular discoveries intrigued Pennypacker. They were not just isolated receipts or bills of sale; they were letters and account books dated during the Revolutionary War and immediately afterward. The handwriting seemed oddly familiar. Pennypacker adjusted his glasses to get a closer look at the distinct way the fourth son of Samuel Townsend, Robert, had hooked his *D*'s and arched his *C*'s. It almost reminded him of—!

Pennypacker rushed to the archives where he stored several letters of espionage that had been signed by members of Washington's secret service during the war. He took a sample from the stack of Robert Townsend's papers next to him and placed it side by side with the Culper Junior letters, peering through a magnifying glass until he was convinced he had a match. Was he holding in his hands clear proof of the identity of the New York spy Washington trusted with his secrets? The reserved, bookish Robert Townsend— perhaps the most private of all the Townsend brothers of his generation—was the daring and courageous Culper Junior!

Of course, Pennypacker needed a professional confirmation of his hunch, so he sent the samples to the nation's leading handwriting analyst. Just a few weeks later, he received a reply. There was no doubt: Oyster Bay, the home of President Teddy Roosevelt, had another hero to celebrate.

With Townsend's identity confirmed, the pieces of the Culper puzzle began to fall into place. The previously disconnected spies now formed a coherent ring, with Townsend at its center. Under the command of Major Benjamin Tallmadge, these five men and one unidentified woman—Robert Townsend, Abraham Woodhull, Austin Roe, Caleb Brewster, James Rivington, and Agent 355—never received the acclaim they deserved in their lifetimes. Together, these men and one woman who had no formal training in the art of espionage, living in Oyster Bay, Setauket, and Manhattan, broke the back of the British military and helped defeat the most powerful fighting force on earth.

One agent remains unidentified: a woman mentioned in the Culper Ring's correspondence by the specific code number 355, "lady." The pages that follow present a compilation of the various activities associated with 355, what history tells us about her probable contributions to the efforts of the Culper Ring, and what resulted from her work. Though her name cannot be verified, and many details about her life are unclear, her presence and her courage undoubtedly made a difference. She represents all covert agents—those men and women whose true identities are never revealed and whose stories are never told, but who offer their service and their lives on behalf of their country. To each of them, we owe an inexpressible debt.

This book recounts the methods, the bravery, the cunning, the near misses, and the incredible successes of the Culper Ring, which helped to save our nation and shape our future. Most of all, this is a story about ordinary citizens doing extraordinary things, people whose fears and hopes and lives were not much different from our own, and how they changed the course of history. Their humility stopped them from seeking fame or fortune because their love of country sparked their exploits.

All Americans owe a tremendous debt of gratitude to George Washington's secret six. This book is written to honor them and the groundwork they laid for our future of freedom.

GEORGE
WASHINGTON'S
SECRET
SIX

Introduction

He was twenty-one years old and knew that in a matter of moments he would die. His request for a clergyman—refused. His request for a Bible—refused. After writing a letter or two to his family, this Yale grad uttered, with dignity, the famous statement "I only regret that I have but one life to lose for my country."

A noose was placed around his neck, and the ladder he had climbed was ripped away. On September 22, 1776, on the island of Manhattan in an area now located at Sixty-Sixth Street and Third Avenue, Captain Nathan Hale was hanged for being a spy. He had volunteered to go behind enemy lines on Long Island for George Washington, and the British would claim that he was caught with sketches of British fortifications and memos of their troop movements. Without a trial, he was sentenced to death. The message sent to all New Yorkers was clear: You spy, you die.

CHAPTER 1

Hold New York, Win the War

New York, without exaggeration, is
the pivot on which the entire
Revolutionary War turns.

—John Adams

The execution of Nathan Hale on September 22, 1776, was the lowest point in a month of low points for General George Washington. First, the British had taken New York City and Long Island— the cornerstones of Washington's strategy because of their valuable geographic and economic positions at the heart of the North American colonies. Now, Washington's attempt at building an intelligence network to recoup that loss had failed spectacularly. Just two months after the fledgling country's declaration of independence, there seemed to be no future for the new nation.

And yet there had been so much hope just a season ago, in spring. After successfully sending the British packing from Boston in March after a prolonged siege, Washington had begun ordering troops toward New York City, whose harbor was of tremendous tactical—and psychological—importance. If the Patriots could hold that other great port of the Northeast, victory might be within reach.

As Washington left Massachusetts on April 4, 1776, to begin his own march southward to rejoin his men, the cheerful reports sent back by the advance parties were confirmed: Farmers and tradesmen were greeting the American troops as they passed through rural villages, pressing gifts of food and drink on the soldiers who had displayed such courage and pluck fighting the redcoats.

"Enjoy this bacon," urged local butchers, heaving slabs of salted meat onto the supply wagons.

"Fresh milk!" announced the housewives who scrambled out of their cottages wielding buckets and dippers.

Gaggles of little boys wearing homespun blue jackets gathered to parade in front of the men as they traversed through town—one child held up a twig as if playing a fife; another pretended to beat a drum in a marching rhythm; the rest chanted the popular refrain "Join or die!" as they reveled in the Patriotic fervor and holiday atmosphere.

Even the sophisticated city crowd, usually much more reserved in their displays of celebration than the country folk, had cheered in the streets as Washington crossed into Providence, Rhode Island. In roadside taverns and stylish urban coffeehouses across Connecticut, toasts were raised to the unlikely homegrown heroes and their quiet but imposing leader. As word spread up the Hudson Valley that the Continental Army was on the move, settlers who now considered themselves Americans, rather than Dutch or German or British subjects, had whispered prayers for the protection and advancement of the cause of independence.

Throughout his nine-day journey spanning four states and nearly three hundred miles of forest roads soggy with springtime mud, Washington had seen increasing hope among the people. There were dissenting voices—those whose closed shutters and drawn shades as the Continental Army passed bespoke their loyalty to King George III and the motherland. But it was clear that there was a sense of growing excitement that this wild, untested experiment in personal freedom and individual rights just might prove more powerful than the most disciplined and well-equipped fighting force on earth.

Despite the buoyant spirits of the people, Washington's own hope was kept in check by a sober view of facts. While the Patriots had enjoyed some early victories in Massachusetts, these wins came at a high cost when compared with their tactical significance. The Battle of Bunker Hill in June 1775, however, had gone to the British, though with heavy loss of life and limb on both sides. The Siege of Boston, which ended the following March, had been a win for the Patriots, but their success was due more to the position and strength of the American fortifications than any great offensive maneuvers to rout the enemy. In the end, the British gave up on the city, leaving voluntarily rather than fleeing in an all-out retreat. General William Howe, commander in chief of the British army in North America, had his sights set on a much bigger and more agreeable prize than belligerent Boston.

New York, tenuously held by a few American troops, was desired by both sides. In the north, the Americans had secured Boston for the moment. To the south, the action had not yet reached a critical point, though its time was coming. Right now, the most pressing concern was in the middle states, where Philadelphia and New York lay vulnerable. Philadelphia was the largest city in the colonies at the time and held great symbolic status as a seat of innovation, boasting one of the first hospitals and public libraries, as well as hosting the meetings of the Continental Congress. Capturing the seat of the fledgling nation's government would be a great victory for the British. And New York City was the linchpin—if the British won it they could bring the colonies to their knees.

As the second-most-populous city in the colonies, New York was their northern economic hub. But even more significant was New York's location and situation—right in the center of Britain's North American settlements and home to both a large deep-water harbor and access to the Hudson River. The army that held New York City and its waterways had a strategic advantage not only in controlling the import and export of foodstuffs and dry goods (which, in turn, affected the economic stability of the region) but also in securing a key foothold for transporting troops up and down the coast.

Maintaining control of New York would give the

American fighting corps and the colonial populace a tremendous boost in confidence. Failing to capture and hold New York City and New York Harbor would certainly be an embarrassment to the British army and navy, but they would survive the blow. For the Americans, however, losing the region would be a tragedy, destroying morale, cutting off trade, and drastically lowering the odds that the Patriots would win the war.

New York's strategic significance, from a trade perspective, was not lost on General Howe. The loss in Massachusetts was a disappointment, but Boston was not the ultimate prize for the British. Howe wanted to choke off the Revolution by isolating the northern colonies from the southern ones. If the political radicals in the somewhat geographically clustered northern cities were segregated from their counterparts in the more spread-out south, they could not cross-pollinate ideologies, and the various factions might be more easily eliminated. It was a classic case of divide and conquer, with New York City as the essential element in creating the chasm.

After regrouping in Halifax, Nova Scotia, following their defeat in Boston, the British set out for New York. On June 29, 1776, three British ships sailed into lower New York Harbor, with General Howe aboard one of them. Both sides knew a battle was imminent.

As Washington marched south in anticipation of Howe's attack, he must have nursed the hope that the Continental Army's muscle and moxie were enough to outfight the British and hold Manhattan. Being a seasoned fighter and a brilliant strategist, he would have understood, perhaps better than anyone else in North America at the time, that control of New York City was essential for the cause of liberty—and that keeping the city would be a daunting task.

Washington and his men arrived in New York in mid-April 1776 and settled in Manhattan. That summer news arrived that both cheered and sobered them. Fifty-six delegates had convened in the midst of stifling July heat in Philadelphia to form the Second Continental Congress, and had forged the Declaration of Independence. If ever there was a point of no return, this was it.

Knowing the attack on New York would not be long delayed, Washington made a short trip to New Jersey and Pennsylvania to meet with his generals. They discussed New York's defenses and supplies—all while trying to anticipate the exact mode of attack. The British, meanwhile, began amassing troops on undefended Staten Island in advance of storming the American positions just across the water in Brooklyn and Manhattan.

As August dragged on, tensions mounted. A copy of the July fourth declaration had been put before the Crown, which meant that King George finally understood the seriousness of the colonists' determination to fight. No longer would King George order his generals to show restraint in their efforts to squelch the rebels or maintain that a mere show of force would be enough to subdue the Revolution. He would not hold back. He would not show mercy. Of this Washington felt sure, and the weight of the "lives, fortunes, and sacred honor" pledged in the name of freedom rested heavily upon his shoulders.

Across the river from Washington, General Henry Clinton had arrived to help lead the attack upon the American positions in New York. As August waned, the British ships loomed large in the harbor, the growing number of redcoats on Staten Island intimidating the sparse American troops.

Faced with an impending attack, Washington sighed one August day as he surveyed the undisciplined, ragtag army at his command in lower Manhattan; his aide-de-camp shifted nervously behind him. The general cleared his throat. "General Howe is rumored to have more than thirty thousand men in the Royal Navy assembled offshore, and twenty thousand men amassed on Staten Island. And we have . . . ?"

His aide was reluctant to reply: "Ten thousand."

If the number was a blow to Washington, he did not show it. Ever the stoic, he refused to allow this dismal news to throw him into despair. Washington was famed as a man who never lost his nerve in battle. The sound of musket fire, the crash of cannonballs, the smell of smoke—none of that seemed to shake his calm, measured way of surveying the chaos and keeping his wits about him as he led his men forward.

But despite Washington's steely nerve, the Americans were in grave trouble. Even substantial numbers of troops meant little without proper training and equipment, and Washington's men lacked both. Washington had the utmost confidence in his officers, but to say that the rank and file of the Continental Army was rough around the edges was an understatement. City men who had never before wielded a rifle stood with country folk who had never had a day of formal schooling. Hardy homesteaders struggled to cooperate with young men of landed wealth who had never known a moment of discomfort or hunger in their lives. Old men lined up with boys who had lied about their age to join the rebels in pursuit of adventure. They came from all over the country: from as far north as the mountains of New Hampshire and as far south as the swamps of Georgia. Many of Washington's men had never before been more than fifty miles from the place of their birth, let alone met anyone with such a strange accent as could be found in the hills of Virginia or the Puritan settlements of Massachusetts. They were all on the side of liberty, but there the unity ended.

Most were brave, to be sure, and loyal—perhaps to a fault. And they were all passionate about their liberty. Washington knew he had the hearts of his men, but whether the passion of an undisciplined few could hold New York against the meticulously trained British forces was another question.

"Hang together or we all hang separately," Washington mused, reciting one of the familiar mantras of the Patriot cause, as he caught a few strains of a bawdy pub song led by the Marylanders sitting around a campfire. All possible preparations against the British onslaught had been made, and he and his men would have to trust it would be enough.

Knowing that an attack was imminent, Washington had made the strategic decision to divide his men into five groups. One had already crossed the harbor to Long Island, and another was stationed in northern

Manhattan to fend off a British encroachment from that direction. The other three groups were situated to defend the lower end of Manhattan. There were several land routes the British might take, but Washington felt confident that all but the least likely and somewhat untraveled route, through Jamaica Pass, were secure. And now . . . they waited.

BETRAYAL AT JAMAICA PASS

The battle was swift and devastating.

Tipped off by someone—whether a spy within Washington's own ranks or a disgruntled Loyalist in New York was unclear—the British learned that Jamaica Pass was guarded by only five men and set out in that direction.

William Howard Jr., a young Patriot who ran a tavern with his father near Jamaica Pass, Long Island, woke about two hours after midnight on the morning of August 27 to a British soldier standing beside his bed. The soldier ordered him to get up, dress, and go downstairs. He quickly obeyed and found his father cornered by three redcoats pointing their muskets with fixed bayonets at him. A glance out the window revealed that a whole fighting unit stood at the ready upon the grounds.

General Howe waited for the two men in the barroom. Sipping a glass of commandeered liquor, he attempted, rather absurdly, to make small talk with the terrified father and son before finally getting to the point. "I must have some one of you to show me over the Rockaway Path around the pass," he remarked, setting down his empty glass.

"We belong to the other side, General," the father replied, "and can't serve you against our duty."

Howe's reply was kind but curt. "That is all very well; stick to your country or stick to your principles when you are free to do so. But tonight, Howard, you are my prisoner, and must guide my men over the hill."

The senior Howard began to protest, but Howe cut him off: "You have no alternative. If you refuse you will be shot."

Shaking, and unaware of just how damaging their compliance would prove, the Howards directed General Howe safely up the winding footpath. Behind them marched ten thousand men through the vulnerable pass, arriving at the other side in time to effectively flank the Patriot general Nathan Woodhull and his men, who were occupied with the frontal assault waged against their defenses in Manhattan when daylight came. As the battle continued throughout the day, Washington recognized his miscalculation that the full contingent of British troops would storm Manhattan—the redcoats were also bringing heavy force to bear on Brooklyn. Washington shifted more men and matériel to Brooklyn, but it was too late for the Americans to recover and hold their ground. By day's end, Brooklyn and the surrounding area was largely in British hands, with the retreating Patriots trapped in Brooklyn Heights. Manhattan alone still held, but Washington was sure it was only a matter of time until the British overtook it, too.

Washington's troops were decimated. All told, the Americans had lost more than 300 men that day, in addition to nearly 700 wounded and 1,000 captured. The British (and their German mercenaries, the Hessians) had lost a mere 64 men, with 31 reported as missing, and 293 wounded.

A MIRACLE IN THE MIST

Things could not have gone more badly for the Continental Army, and both sides knew it. And it wasn't over, though the cannons had ceased to fire. The fighting had taken Washington across the East River, but now he was essentially trapped in Brooklyn Heights, surrounded by the British and with no way to escape. If his troops pursued a retreat by land, they would walk directly into the British camps and be either shot on sight or captured and hanged for treason. If they took to the water to escape to Patriot-held Manhattan, they would be sitting ducks as the British fired cannonballs into the rowboats. Then again, that was likely too messy—the British prided themselves on their extreme pragmatism. No, they would probably take the more gentlemanly route of allowing their marksmen to pick off the retreating Americans one by one.

Just like that, the Revolution was all but over. Washington must have reeled at the turn of events. Maybe it was inevitable; after all, who were the colonists to think they had a chance against the mighty king of England and an empire that encircled the globe? Washington had been entrusted with the hopes, dreams, lives, and futures of every American Patriot—and he was standing on the brink of failure.

The Americans needed to get out and get out fast. If the bedraggled and punch-drunk Patriot soldiers could somehow manage to escape, they could regroup with the friendly troops waiting in American-controlled territory. It was a big "if."

"We have no other options?" Washington asked the officers assembled with him at his makeshift headquarters in Brooklyn Heights.

There was a pause as each man looked around the table with raised eyebrows, as if asking his comrades, "Have *you* got any miracles to spare?"

But Washington already knew the answer. Unless he could somehow ferry nine thousand men undetected across New York Harbor, currently patrolled by the might of the Royal Navy, he would be forced to surrender or ask his men to die in a siege from which there was no foreseeable escape. And with the betrayal regarding their vulnerability at Jamaica Pass, and no individual able to convey intelligence from the British positions, there was no way to anticipate what the redcoats' next move might be.

Washington was near despair, but he was also a man of faith. No one knows what prayers passed his lips during those tense two days as he faced almost certain defeat. As night fell on the evening of August 29, he peered over New York Harbor and knew he had no other hope. Escape by water was the only chance—and even that would take a miracle. Ordering a hasty retreat, Washington oversaw the efforts to ferry his army and their possessions—every man, beast, cannon, and rifle—safely across the water under the cover of darkness. To his relief, the British sentinels failed to spot the shadowy silhouettes of the escaping soldiers. But as the sky began to lighten, there were still men to move—and it was then that Washington's prayers proved effective. A thick fog began to roll in, like the benevolent breath of God, providing cover and protection until every last soldier and piece of equipment reached safety on the other side. Washington's boots were the last to leave the Brooklyn Heights side of the harbor, and the last to alight in Manhattan, which the Patriots still held.

By the time the fog had fully lifted and the British realized what had happened, the Americans were already out of the reach of British cannons. They were down, but not out—though just barely. Washington knew it would be only a matter of days before General Howe ordered an attack on the remaining American fortifications in Manhattan, which would surely fall.

Moving north to Connecticut, Washington and his men rejoiced in their escape, though the all-but-complete loss of New York was a serious blow. Gone was the optimism created by the Boston victory. Troop morale was low. Backed into a corner, Washington now realized what every small child comes to recognize when faced with the brute strength of a school-yard bully: He could not defeat his foe with manpower, arms, or any other show of force. He would have to beat the British in a battle of wits.

CHAPTER 2

The Need for a Spy Ring

As if the loss of most of New York weren't bad enough, Washington's autumn was about to get worse. While the defeat at the Battle of Brooklyn had been a blow, the retreat had gone better than planned. Washington's next endeavor would not be so fortunate, ending instead in disaster.

The few American troops still holding Manhattan were hanging on by a thread, and Washington was desperate to strengthen their position. To do so, he would need a spy to collect information on British plans. Espionage was not a new activity to Washington. Having fought in the French and Indian War and served as a spy himself, he understood the roots of the present conflict—an insight that would frame his use of an intelligence network in the Revolution.

THE FRENCH AND INDIAN WAR

Two decades earlier, in 1754, the British army (consisting of both soldiers from the motherland and local colonial militias) had launched a war in North America against the French army and native tribes who were attacking British citizens in regions granted in previous treaties to the British government. For the next nine years, the continent was embroiled in battles to control the various outposts and forts sprinkled across the wilderness regions of the Ohio River and Appalachian Mountains.

The previous year, Washington, just twenty-one years old, volunteered to engage with the French soldiers and learn whatever he could about their intentions and fortifications through leading conversations, as well as whatever was carelessly shared over wine bottles. As it did throughout his life, Washington's temperate nature had served him well on that mission; he maintained his sobriety and clearheadedness so that he could report back to his superiors that the French had no intentions of quitting the country without a fight.

This conflict, in which Washington came of age, was part of the international unrest rooted in ancient rivalries and grudges resurrected by modern ambitions. But world attitudes had changed following the Treaty of Paris in 1763, and Washington's role would change, too. France's claims to its overseas colonies were devastated. Britain gained several of France's North American colonies along the northern Atlantic and in the Caribbean, as well as the Florida territory held by Spain. People suddenly found themselves subject to a new crown and a new flag—sometimes even those of a former enemy. For the American colonists, who had long been subjects of the king of England (despite their Dutch, German, Irish, Scottish, Welsh, or West African ancestry) and necessarily viewed his enemies as their own, the expulsion of the French and Spanish from bordering regions lifted much of their fear of invasion and need for protection. Now they could focus more on their own interests. Recognizing that their rights and freedoms were being neither defended nor advanced by the king they had faithfully served, they began to rebel against the very government they had once relied upon for security.

ACTS OF AGGRESSION

In 1764, the British Parliament determined that the cost of the French and Indian War had been too high. Troops remained stationed in the colonies, adding to the financial strain, so additional revenues were needed to pay for their presence, as well as to tighten trade restrictions on the colonies. Over the next few years, Parliament voted to levy a series of taxes against the American colonists. The Sugar Act and the Currency Act restricted trade and the issuance of colonial money. Then Parliament expanded its reach in 1765 with the Stamp Act, which required that all printed matter—newspapers, legal contracts, pamphlets—must be produced with paper from London and embossed with a seal of verification.

This action was, in itself, not unreasonable—the colonists could be expected to help pay for their own defense. But the independent-minded colonists reacted angrily because of the act's broader implications. All English citizens were supposed to be afforded the right of representation in Parliament, but there were no members of Parliament for the American colonies to agree to the taxation and insist that it be reasonable. The cry of "no taxation without representation" was sounded, and a Stamp Act Congress convened in New York City in October 1765 to protest the measure. The Stamp Act was eventually repealed, but others followed in its wake as King George continued to expand the power and grasp of the Crown, while simultaneously diminishing the rights of his colonial subjects.

In March 1770, the so-called Boston Massacre illustrated just how high tensions were running. British soldiers fired into a crowd of protesting Americans, killing five and wounding six. After the grassroots Sons of Liberty staged their famous Boston Tea Party in December 1773, dumping 342 chests of tea into Boston Harbor, London responded the following spring with harsh laws designed to make an example of Massachusetts as a warning to the other colonies not to challenge the Crown's authority.

The warning was heard loud and clear, but it did not quell the fires of rebellion as Parliament had hoped. In fact, it had the opposite effect. In response to the Intolerable Acts, as the laws had been dubbed by the Americans, the First Continental Congress met in Philadelphia in September and October of 1774. Fifty-six men representing twelve of the thirteen colonies (Georgia opted not to attend) voted to unite in a series of boycotts against British goods; prominent Patriots, including Thomas Jefferson, Patrick Henry, and Henry Lee, were among the outspoken dissenters. They also resolved to send a petition of their grievances to King George in a last effort to prevent an escalation of hostilities.

The petition went unanswered. In April 1775, combat broke out between colonists and British troops at Lexington and Concord in Massachusetts; the following month, the Second Continental Congress convened to prepare for a full-scale war. Among the delegates from Virginia was the tall, soft-spoken surveyor, farmer, and former spy widely regarded for his valor in battle and exemplary leadership in the militia during the previous war: George Washington.

HOW TO WIN A WAR

Following his brief stint as a spy, Washington had led thousands of troops into battle, riding tall and remaining calm through even the heaviest bombardment. Later myths grew up around Washington—that he was spoken of in native prophesies as a man favored by the gods, that no arrows could touch him. If not actually invincible, he was at least regarded as unflappable by his peers, a sober-minded man of vision, wisdom, humility, and experience. For these reasons Washington was asked to serve as the commander in chief of the Continental Army. Now, two decades after his first spying mission, he would be engaged in a battle of his own to drive from that same land the British government he had once faithfully served. Who could have imagined such an outcome? But life was a strange pageant; he understood that well enough. And Washington knew that espionage would play a more important role in this new war.

In traditional wars that pitted monarch against monarch, there was a mutual respect for the authority of the crown even if there was a deep hatred for the person who wore it or the land claims he or she recognized. In those battles, it was all about might; the armies fought until someone was finally overpowered. Or, as had happened so often in new territories, one army fought with weapons, manpower, disease— whatever they had—until the other population was simply eradicated. Washington quickly realized that this revolution was different. King George respected no one and recognized no authority, certainly not whatever makeshift government the colonies could cobble together. His increasingly oppressive laws and his silence in the face of organized protests had made that clear. Yet the king would not seek to completely decimate the population of the colonies; dead subjects cannot pay taxes.

No, this war would be different from any other that had come before it. Of that Washington felt sure. It would not be a fight to the death, nor could it be simply a clash of armies. If the Americans wanted to emerge victorious from this conflict, they would not try to overpower their enemy; they would simply refuse to back down or go away. They didn't need to be conquering heroes—they just needed to survive.

As New York slipped from his grasp, Washington saw that the Patriots would need to outmaneuver, not overpower, the enemy. And, by learning the enemy's secrets, spies would play a crucial role in undermining British attacks through anticipating the redcoats' next moves. It would be the only way to counter the superior numbers, training, supplies, and equipment of the British army and navy. This was especially true in the more populous cities, where the enemy had stationed large pockets of troops. There was little hope of defeating the British in head-to-head combat unless their battle plans and their weaknesses were already known.

Unfortunately for the rough-hewn Patriot army, spying required far more accuracy and delicacy than simply aiming a cannon, and it also took more time. Unlike waging a traditional battle, wherein two armies took to a field and fired at each other for several hours or days until one side declared victory, gathering useful intelligence might take weeks or months before combat even began. Developing the sophistication and buying the time necessary to grow an effective spy ring would be difficult—especially in the locations where it mattered most.

Recognizing the difficulty of setting up a good espionage network, Washington began converting his wartime strategy from relying on nonexistent combat strength to placing his trust in intelligence gathering even before the catastrophic loss of New York was complete. To begin, he needed one good man.

NATHAN HALE STEPS FORWARD

Captain Nathan Hale felt his heart leap when he learned of General Washington's request that September. The general needed a man to venture behind enemy lines disguised as a Loyalist. He would make casual inquiries and investigations into the troop movements and supply stores and report back to Washington. His work would inform the general's plans to take back New York City, its harbor, and the neighboring areas.

Lieutenant Colonel Thomas Knowlton had assembled a select group of officers to inform them of the need. Each was brave, each was trustworthy, and each was silent as he stood before them asking for a volunteer. Finally, twenty-one-year-old Nathan Hale stepped forward.

"Are you a native of Long Island?" Colonel Knowlton questioned the eager young man as they met in Knowlton's makeshift office to discuss the particulars of the mission.

"No, sir. Coventry, Connecticut, and from there to Yale College."

"Then you must have visited Long Island as a boy?"

"No, sir. I have never been, though I do have some distant cousins there." Hale neglected to add that those cousins were Loyalists, rightly assuming such information would give no boost to his petition.

"Have you even a passing familiarity with the land? Perhaps from studying its geography or the surveyors' charts?"

"Well, sir, my good friend from college, Lieutenant Benjamin Tallmadge, often urged me to visit his family there during the summer and sometimes showed me on maps where his home was located and which were the best coves for watching the ships come in."

"Nothing more?"

"No, sir."

The colonel shifted in his camp chair. This interview was growing uncomfortable. "How did you occupy your time at Yale?"

"With my studies, astronomy, debates—and theatricals, sir."

Theatricals. Well, that was something, Knowlton thought. At least Hale would have some ability to assume a role and play it convincingly. Then again, he also knew that college plays tended to be either overwrought classical dramas of the Greeks and Romans or else hilarious farces featuring boisterous young actors more interested in laughing as their friends donned ladies' dresses and wigs than in conveying any part of an intelligible story.

"I see that your unit of the Connecticut militia participated in the victorious Siege of Boston last year; am I correct to assume, then, that you are a seasoned soldier acquainted with the deprivations of supplies and the stress of battle?"

Hale blinked rapidly and color rose in his face. "No, sir. I was a schoolmaster in New London and my teaching contract did not end until that July. The siege was already over by the time I was released from my obligations. I have been involved in some small actions, but nothing of much significance. However"—he fumbled in his pocket and drew out a letter—"Lieutenant Tallmadge took it upon himself to write to me last summer when I was preparing to leave the school and join up with the Seventh Connecticut Regiment, and his words . . . well, they inspired me, sir."

The older man eyed Hale warily. That Tallmadge was a rising star in the Continental Army was undeniable, but Tallmadge's own shrewdness and ability did not automatically transfer to his idealistic young friend. "What did he say that could have possibly stirred your soul so much that you would volunteer to be the lone operative in a dangerous mission?"

"With your permission, sir?" Hale held up the letter.

Knowlton nodded.

"'I am informed that you are honored by the Assembly with a Lieutenant's commission,'" Hale began reading in a clear, strong voice that both surprised and impressed his lone audience member. Maybe the young man had been a promising thespian on the Yale stage after all. "'I think the more extensive Service would be my choice. Our holy Religion, the honour of our God, a glorious country, & a happy constitution is what we have to defend. Some indeed may say there are others who may supply your place. True there are men who would gladly accept such a proposal but are we certain that they would be likely to answer just as good an end? . . . We all should be ready to step forth in the common cause.'"

The taper on the wax candle atop Knowlton's desk sputtered a little as tiny flecks of ash fell onto the wood;

otherwise, the room was silent. He weighed the conflicting thoughts in his mind. Hale certainly seemed intelligent, if wet behind the ears, and his conviction was undeniable and moving—inspiring, even. True, he knew nothing of Long Island, but a quick study on local geography and customs would be sufficient. Besides, who else had stepped up? There were no other volunteers as far as he knew, and Washington needed his man as quickly as possible. "You truly believe you can do this?"

"I have no doubt, sir, that I am the right man."

"And you have no concerns about espionage being a breach of honor?"

Hale took a deep breath, then voiced a sentiment he had clearly been mulling for some time: "I wish to be useful, and every kind of service necessary to the public good becomes honorable by being necessary. If the exigencies of my country demand a peculiar service, its claims to the performance of that service are imperious."

Knowlton hid a smile at the earnestness of this prepared speech but had to admire Hale's seriousness. "How soon can you travel, Lieutenant?"

Hale grinned. "Right away, sir."

"I shall inform General Washington of the fact, and of your eagerness to undertake the task at hand." Colonel Knowlton rose to his feet, closing the interview. "Speak to no one of our meeting. You will be called upon in due time if needed. You are dismissed."

With a sharp salute, Hale turned on his heel and strode buoyantly out the door.

AN ARMY OF ONE

Washington immediately approved Hale's assignment. On September 12, the young man was ferried across the water from Stamford, Connecticut, to Long Island. He would pose as a schoolmaster looking for work, a cover that would give him an excuse to meet leading townsmen and ask questions about the area.

But the move was too late. As September advanced, so had the British troops, capturing the lower end of Manhattan on September 15, just three days after Hale landed. The defeat had been inevitable and Washington was prepared for the blow, but the timing could not have been worse.

Hale had little chance to establish his identity, let alone transmit any helpful intelligence to Washington, before the attack came and changed the entire purpose of his mission. Instead of gathering clues for how the Americans might defend their last stronghold, he now had to equip them with the knowledge of how they might win back the city. Washington feared the fledgling spy would not be able to adapt.

Not that Washington hadn't been impressed with Hale. Quite the opposite, in fact. The passion, boldness, and just a touch of cockiness that Hale had demonstrated seemed to Washington to perfectly encapsulate the Patriot movement. But just as many questioned the wisdom of the Americans' challenge to the British Crown, Washington, too, found himself wondering whether Hale's fervor, while certainly admirable, was not also a little naive. Did he really know what he was getting into? Then again, did any of them? The Americans had yanked the lion's mane, and now Hale had walked into one of its lairs.

Washington felt keenly the responsibility for Hale's safety, having had the final say on whether or not the mission would go forward. There was no way of knowing how the young man was coping, and this concerned Washington even more. Where was he staying? With whom was he speaking? Had he stumbled into any situations that might put him in harm's way—more so than the mission itself, that is? Every time he heard the rapid hooves of a post-rider's horse, he had to fight the urge to run out and seize the letters from the courier's hands. Just as much as he craved the information Hale would be sending, Washington wanted the assurance that the young lieutenant still maintained his cover and felt confident in his ability to quietly exit Long Island when the right moment came.

Long Island was enemy territory. Its farmland crawled with soldiers determined to hold on to their slice of land and eager to arrest anyone who might threaten their prospects of gaining more. Because the British were so firmly entrenched in their prize real estate, it was a perfect holding pen for the British army awaiting the next offensive strike, and the troops poured in. By the time Hale landed, the island was full of redcoats armed and itching for a fight with anyone who had even a whiff of Patriot sentiments about him.

But just as potentially damning to Hale's mission was the civilian population. While a few Patriots suffered through the occupation, the sympathies of most Long Islanders lay with King George. Even if a farmer was a Patriot, with a British military officer taking quarter in his house he was very likely to shout "God save the king!" if it kept his children safe and his fields unscathed. For this reason alone, Washington worried that a seemingly trustworthy contact might be tempted to report a suspected spy, whether out of true loyalty to the Crown or in the hopes of procuring some additional protection for his own family and property.

Any number of innocent situations could blow Hale's cover to a suspicious local: an ignorance of the proximity of one town to the next, the mispronunciation of a word peculiar to that region, a slip of the tongue that betrayed him as a mainlander. The flimsy nature of Hale's cover story might easily be blown as well—what school would be looking for a teacher this far into September? Perhaps he might be spotted by an old friend and hailed with a familiarity that would be impossible to deny. A Loyalist relative might do the same thing, but with less innocent intentions. Or maybe even Hale's own Patriotic zeal would do him in, were he unable to remain silent in the face of insults to his cause or so trusting that he shared his true feelings with someone masquerading as a sympathetic ear.

A week passed with no disaster, and Washington breathed a sigh of relief. While the danger was still intense, he hoped Hale had established a solid cover and was out of direct suspicion. Unfortunately, his relief was premature.

FAILURE

On September 21, Washington spent most of the day studying maps and potential battle plans and, in the evening, writing a few letters. He had no way of knowing that at the tip of the peninsula, Nathan Hale was, at that very moment, being arrested, charged with spying, and sentenced to "be hanged by the neck until dead" the following morning.

As if to highlight Hale's lonely experience on Long Island, no one can say with certainty exactly where he was detected and captured, or even what activities he was engaged in before that fateful event. Somehow he made his way westward to Brooklyn, then crossed over into lower Manhattan, though no records show exactly when or how. Perhaps he only made that crossing later, as a prisoner. By some reports, he was recognized by some Loyalist cousins and reported to the British; by other reports, he mistook a British boat as the ferry sent to return him to safety; by still others, he was lulled into a false sense of security and shared the details of his plans with some Loyalist locals at a tavern and they turned him in. Whatever the case, he was captured, tried, and hanged all in the span of roughly twelve hours.

Shortly after Hale's body ceased to swing like a pendulum in the Park of Artillery, Captain John Montresor of His Majesty's army set out for the American camp under a flag of truce. He was granted an audience with a young Patriot captain and aide to General Washington named Alexander Hamilton to explain the purpose of his visit and inform the Americans of the execution of Lieutenant Hale. The visit was not only a formal courtesy but also a thinly veiled warning that their sad little attempt at espionage had been an embarrassing failure.

The news cut Washington deeply. Casualties were an unavoidable part of the ugly business of war, but had the general not known the futility of the effort even before sending Hale on his mission? Had he not immediately detected a dozen problems with the plan? Did he not sense, deep down, that it had been doomed from the start when one brave but untried young man had taken all of the responsibility upon himself? Hale's death was a tragedy for its own sake, for the fact that Washington now had no agent to feed him the information he desperately needed from Long Island, and because of how unnecessary it was. Had there only been a more knowledgeable, less conspicuous ring in place whose members could not only gather the necessary information but also protect one another even as they operated in anonymity, things might have gone very differently.

Hale's attempt to gather and convey information had been an utter failure, but he had given his beloved general something just as valuable: the recognition that Washington needed more than just one brave man on Long Island; he needed an entire network.

A TURN AT TRENTON

As the autumn of 1776 progressed to winter, General George Washington found himself marching from

New York to New Jersey to Pennsylvania in a series of disheartening campaigns. His troops were demoralized and the civilian population even more so, as many who were formerly enthusiastic supporters of the Patriotic cause took oaths of fidelity to the king or else simply quietly withdrew their support for liberty. In October, Washington met up with reinforcements, but found their number a mere half of the five thousand troops he had anticipated. Supplies were low and he could no longer count on the local populace to show their support by selling food and other necessary supplies to the Continental Army. The British troops, on the other hand, were well supplied and their numbers bolstered by the Hessians, German mercenaries with a reputation for being boulders of men and unflappable in battle.

Just before the celebration of Christmas, Washington was eyeing a return to New Jersey. He had to regain control of the mid-Atlantic after the disappointing autumn or lose the war, so he began to formulate a plan to attack the Hessian encampment at Trenton—a daring raid requiring yet another treacherous ferrying of men and supplies across water. Braving large masses of ice and winter winds that could easily overturn the small boats, his men would cross the river and capture the city in an attempt to break a stronghold of British control in the region.

"We are in a very disaffected part of the Provence," Washington wrote to his brothers John and Samuel in two telling and very nearly verbatim letters. Samuel's version, dated December 18, 1776, reads:

And between you and me, I think our Affairs are in a very bad situation; not so much from the apprehension of Genl. Howe's Army, as from the defection of New York, Jerseys, and Pennsylvania. In short, the Conduct of the Jerseys has been most Infamous. Instead of turning out to defend their Country and affording aid to our Army, they are making their submissions as fast as they can. If the Jerseys had given us any support, we might have made a stand at Hackensack and after that at Brunswick, but the few Militia that were in Arms, disbanded themselves or slunk off in such a manner upon the appearance of danger as to leave us quite unsupported and to make the best shifts we could without them and left the poor remains of our Army to make the best we could of it.

I have no doubt but that General Howe will still make an attempt upon Philadelphia this Winter. I see nothing to oppose him a fortnight hence, as the time of all the Troops, except those of Virginia (reduced almost to nothing,) and Smallwood's Regiment of Maryland, (equally as bad) will expire in less than that time. In a word my dear Sir, if every nerve is not strain'd to recruit the New Army with all possible expedition, I think the game is pretty near up. . . .

You can form no Idea of the perplexity of my Situation. No Man, I believe, ever had a

greater choice of difficulties and less means to
extricate himself from them. However under a
full persuasion of the justice of our Cause I
cannot but think the prospect will brighten, al-
though for a wise purpose it is, at present hid
under a cloud entertain an Idea that it will fi-
nally sink tho' it may remain for some time
under a Cloud.

Washington had smiled a little, in spite of himself, as he closed the letter with greetings sent to his sister-in-law and her children. Yes, the past few months had been bleak and the future looked like it would be very much the same, but Washington clung to that shred of hope with which he had reassured his brother. Though the Patriot cause was cloaked by a cloud, his cautious optimism was rooted in something more solid than just a desperate hope that another miracle may yet come to his aid. Washington had a secret.

John Honeyman, a Scots-Irish immigrant who had served the British Crown faithfully during the French and Indian War, was now plying his trade as a weaver and butcher in Trenton, supplying the Hessian troops and making his allegiance to the Crown common knowledge. While wandering dangerously close to the American lines one day, Honeyman had been captured and questioned by none other than General Washington himself. A few days later, shortly after Washington had written to his brothers, Honeyman escaped back to Trenton under the cover of some small disturbance in the camp. Once again behind Hessian lines, he insisted upon an audience with Colonel Johann Rall, informing him of what he had observed while held by the Americans.

"There will be no attack," Honeyman told Rall. "The American troops are so disheartened and so bedraggled, they have no plans of advancing any time soon."

The big German laughed at the thought of the upstart colonials wasting away as they tried to put on a brave show: "Wir werden fröhliches Weihnachten schließlich haben!" (We will have a merry Christmas, after all!)

Colonel Rall dismissed the trusted tradesman with a hearty slap on the back, and went to inform his subordinates that they could stand down and commence with the Christmas celebrations. Someone had procured quite a few casks of ale, and they were all eager to toast the birth of the Christ child in roaring fashion even as the church tolled the bells marking Christmas Eve. Meanwhile, Honeyman quickly and quietly gathered his family and retreated eastward to New Brunswick, New Jersey . . . and Washington prepared to strike.

It had all been a beautifully orchestrated setup, from Honeyman's position in Trenton to his capture, escape, and meeting with Rall. He had been a dedicated British soldier twenty years ago, but now he was Washington's man. Learning from Hale's death, the general had reached out to Honeyman earlier that fall, counting on his outstanding credentials from the previous war, unshakable bravery, and unsuspicious occupation to enable him to operate undetected. Sure enough, Honeyman casually questioned and carefully counted the men about the city and offered a full report of it back to Washington from his jail cell following his "capture." Washington, having personally arranged for the means by which Honeyman could escape, had then asked his agent to plant the false story in Rall's ear before spiriting himself and his family out of harm's way when the attack came on the unsuspecting Hessians.

It was a perfect plan that went off without a hitch. Honeyman played his part beautifully, and the Hessian troops, all fighting massive hangovers from their raucous Christmas revelries, were caught completely off guard when the Patriots launched their attack in the wee hours of December 26. The victory was swift, decisive, and crucial for the American cause.

Washington's espionage success further buoyed him and the troops. But the loss of Long Island and Manhattan still weighed heavily on the general's mind. He didn't think the war could be won without recapturing them and, like Trenton, they could not be taken without good, reliable intelligence. Honeyman's efforts at Trenton had proved the value of a well-placed spy and taught two good lessons: Washington's spies would have to blend in as Honeyman had (and Hale had not), and they would have to be absolutely convincing in their roles.

Washington would need a collection of agents—a ring of common men and women with unquestionable fidelity and unassuming identities. His first task would be to enlist two key individuals: (1) an officer familiar with the territory and well acquainted with the local families and customs, who could orchestrate the whole enterprise but remain close to Washington's side, and (2) an agent on the ground who could recruit the other members, preferably a person who was well connected but had largely kept his political opinions to himself throughout the conflict thus far—a man who would not raise suspicions but would rather die than surrender his God-given liberties.

CHAPTER 3

Launching the Ring

In February 1777, Washington wrote to Nathaniel Sackett, a New York merchant, supplier to the Continental Army, and Patriot activist. The short letter got to the heart of the matter immediately. He offered Sackett fifty dollars a month—a generous sum from the cash-strapped American government—to establish a network of spies to learn "the earliest and best intelligence of the designs of the enemy." Sackett's efforts, while initially fruitful, collapsed a few months later in a series of unfortunate mishaps and failed missions that yielded few results of the impact Washington was seeking. Finding the right man to lead the New York ring was proving harder than planned.

In the fall of 1777, a year after Nathan Hale's death, Washington still had no New York spy ring, mostly because the general's attentions were diverted again from New York to Philadelphia, which the British had recently captured. For the next few months, Washington devoted most of his attention to regaining the City of

Brotherly Love and placed the New York intelligence efforts on hold indefinitely.

A MISSION

As 1777 turned into 1778, the tide of the war changed. When Benjamin Franklin's negotiations in France finally culminated in Louis XVI's commitment to support the American cause in February 1778, the British strategy had to change. Despite a devastating winter at Valley Forge, the Americans were no longer fighting alone, scraping out victories from sheer luck, pluck, and whatever good fortune Providence threw their way. By June 1778, orders were issued for the British army in Philadelphia to abandon the city and set their sights on strengthening their all-important hold on New York.

Washington and his men prepared to follow suit, packing up the ragtag army to leave Valley Forge. The logistics of moving an army were all-consuming, but Washington was preoccupied with an even more important task—the time had come to focus his full attention on forming his spy network, and nothing would distract him now.

Washington tapped Brigadier General Charles Scott, a rustic man from central Virginia, to serve as his chief of intelligence. It was a logical appointment; Scott was experienced and able, with an impressive record in command. He had distinguished himself as a scout during the French and Indian War and had served alongside Washington for the duration of the

Pennsylvania campaign. But despite Scott's capabilities and qualifications, he was abrasive and unimaginative. Even worse, his knowledge of the topography and waterways of Manhattan and Long Island was severely limited.

Quickly recognizing that Scott's efforts could easily go the same way as Nathan Hale's and Nathaniel Sackett's, Washington scrambled to find another man to head up the actual infiltration of New York. He needed someone who knew not only the city and the various routes into and out of it but also enough trusted locals to recruit as spies. The candidate would also need to be nearly inexhaustible if he were to devote the time, strategy, and energy necessary to make the ring successful.

Fortunately for Washington, one of the rising young stars of the Continental Army fit the bill exactly. Benjamin Tallmadge, a gallant young major whose curls always seemed to be escaping beneath his sharp dragoon helmet, was still rather green, but his keenness of mind was apparent to everyone who met him, and he knew how to earn the respect and faith of his men despite the occasional misstep. Besides, his demonstrated courage, his imagination, and, most important, his background made him the perfect candidate.

A RISING STAR

Major Benjamin Tallmadge was a rather unlikely military man. He was born on February 25, 1754, the second son of the Reverend Benjamin and Susannah Smith

Tallmadge, in a parsonage in Setauket, a hamlet in the region of Brookhaven, Suffolk County, Long Island. The son and grandson of a minister, young Benjamin seemed destined for the pulpit rather than the trenches.

Benjamin Junior was an extremely bright, precocious child. One of his father's duties as parson was to instruct the young men of the village who were hoping to attend college, preparing them for the rigorous entrance exams by supplying them with the requisite knowledge of Latin, Greek, theology, and rhetoric. Energetic and enthusiastic about anything that seemed remotely challenging, young Benjamin was eager to join his father's classes and thrived under increasingly difficult curricula. By the age of twelve or thirteen, he had proved so proficient that he was admitted to Yale by the college president, but the Reverend Tallmadge felt his son was too young. At his father's bidding, Benjamin waited until he was fifteen to enroll. In the meantime, Susannah died, leaving the Tallmadge men alone in the parsonage. The sadness in the house following her passing was oppressive, and Benjamin found that leaving was something of a relief.

He was well prepared for college life. "Being so well versed in the Latin and Greek languages, I had not much occasion to study during the first two years of my collegiate life," Tallmadge later admitted, "which I have always thought had a tendency to make me idle." But his time was not wasted. He quickly became popular among his classmates, including Nathan Hale, who found Tallmadge's intelligence, energy, and good nature fascinating.

Playhouses were very rare in the colonies at the time, and public opinion considered theater somewhere between frivolous and downright sinful. This irresistible combination of novelty and potential scandal made theatricals a favorite pastime among college students. Tallmadge and Hale were often at the center of these productions, and frequented several other clubs that explored the various disciplines future schoolmasters should master: astronomy, geometry, history, debate, and natural sciences. These subjects were also covered in classes, but this was the Age of Enlightenment and the pursuit of knowledge was all the rage—even among fun-loving young men.

Benjamin graduated from Yale in 1773 with a distinguished academic record, despite his somewhat lackadaisical freshman and sophomore years, and a severe bout of measles that marked part of his junior and senior years; he was even invited by the college president to speak at the commencement ceremony. Upon graduation, the position of superintendent of the high school in Wethersfield, Connecticut, was offered to him, and Tallmadge seized the opportunity to impart his enthusiasm for study to a younger generation. There, he served faithfully for three years, though his ambitions drew him toward the legal profession and he began to seriously consider studying law.

But in the spring of 1775, "the shot heard 'round the world" rang out at Lexington, Massachusetts, followed by a skirmish at Concord a few hours later. That one day, April 19, would mark an indelible change in the course of history, and Benjamin Tallmadge, like many other young men of his time, was swept up in Patriotic fervor as the War of Independence officially began. The bloody battle at Bunker Hill raged shortly afterward in June, and Tallmadge took advantage of his school's summer holiday to ride the one hundred miles to Boston to learn of the latest news firsthand. He met with some Connecticut friends who had been involved in the combat, and their stories of heroism and zeal began to shift Tallmadge's goal from fighting injustice in the courtroom to fighting tyranny on the battlefield.

He began the fall term at Wethersfield seriously weighing various courses for his future. With the arrival of 1776, the Continental Congress gave approval for the colonies to actively expand their fighting brigades. Captain John Chester, one of the friends with whom Tallmadge had visited the previous summer, was elevated to the rank of colonel, and invited Tallmadge to join his regiment as a commissioned officer. Thus, Lieutenant Benjamin Tallmadge, his commission signed by Governor Jonathan Trumbull, took his leave of the school at the end of the term and officially became a member of Connecticut's Continental Line on June 20, 1776.

It was a move that astonished Benjamin's father and his second wife, the former Miss Zipporah Strong. As his unit marched toward Manhattan, Lieutenant Tallmadge gained leave to venture across the water to Long Island to see his family. His pious father was shocked to learn that both Benjamin and his older son, William, had enlisted, but he granted his blessing at Benjamin's request.

Now a soldier, Tallmadge continued to distinguish himself with his boundless energy and uncanny knack for winning people over, but the art of war didn't come easily to the new recruit. With August came the fateful Battle of Brooklyn and the betrayal of Brigadier General Nathaniel Woodhull and his branch of the Long Island militia at Jamaica Pass. The battle was Tallmadge's first taste of war, and it shook him.

"This was the first time in my life that I had witnessed the awful scene of a battle, when man was engaged to destroy his fellow-man," Tallmadge wrote more than fifty years later. "I well remember my sensations on the occasion, for they were solemn beyond description, and very hardly could I bring my mind to be willing to attempt the life of a fellow-creature."

Their father's blessing proved fruitful for Benjamin but not for his brother William. At the same time that Benjamin was experiencing such a conflict of conscience at the horror of killing, William was being hauled off as a prisoner, captured in battle by the British. In the desperate weeks that followed, Benjamin's good nature and dogged determination failed him for perhaps the first time in his life. Together with some influential friends, he made repeated attempts to have provisions delivered to William in the British prison ship where he was being held, but all efforts were rebuffed, all food parcels and blankets denied. William starved to death at some point in the autumn of 1776, and his body was either thrown over the side of the ship into cold New York Harbor or buried in an unmarked grave on the shore.

Nathan Hale's death, coinciding with William's desperate plight, was a difficult blow. Tallmadge's conscience shouted that he would have been a far better man for the job than poor Hale, who had never even set foot on Long Island. But the opportunity had not been offered to Tallmadge and he had precious little time to dwell on the tragedy. His unit continued to march with General Washington, engaging in the Battle of White Plains on October 28, when Benjamin himself was very nearly captured by Hessian troops as he was ushering his men across the river.

In mid-December 1776, Benjamin Tallmadge was appointed captain of the Second Continental Light Dragoons by General George Washington himself, who had admired the young man's abilities and conduct, not to mention his loyalty. The appointment was signed in the unmistakable hand of John Hancock, and Tallmadge accepted it willingly. He devoted the first third of 1777 to training men and horses for reconnaissance, scouting missions, and light raids ahead of the more heavily armed cavalry and artillery brigades, a job, Tallmadge later wrote, that he enjoyed thoroughly: "My own troop was composed entirely of *dapple gray horses,* which, with black straps and black bear-skin holster-covers, looked superb. I have no hesitation in acknowledging that I was very proud of this command."

Tallmadge continued his dedicated and distinguished service, and a promotion to major followed in April 1777. At the end of that year, something happened that would change his career. After an attack on his troops, Tallmadge received word of an unusual nature. As he described it, "a *country girl* had gone into Philadelphia; with eggs, instructed to obtain some information respecting the enemy." Arrangements were made that she should meet Tallmadge at the Rising Sun Tavern, where she quickly passed on all information about troop numbers and supply counts that she had been able to gather, likely from another sympathetic contact inside the city.

But the Rising Sun was not an ideal place for cover, as it was clearly visible from the British lines, and Tallmadge was spotted and identified entering the establishment. While the girl was still offering her report, the alarm was sounded that an armed British guard was fast approaching; Tallmadge dashed outside, swung the girl up behind him on his horse, and the two took off at full speed, streaking toward Germantown, a little more than three miles away, with the British in close pursuit. Once in the safety of town, the girl dismounted and disappeared, and Tallmadge began to make his way back to his unit.

But the experience of the young citizen-spy stayed with him. "During the whole ride," he recorded in his memoirs, "although there was considerable firing of pistols, and not a little wheeling and charging, she remained unmoved, and never once complained for fear after she mounted my horse. I was delighted with this transaction, and received many compliments from those who became acquainted with it."

Bravery and resolve from the most unlikely corners could still be counted on to rise to the challenge and take on whatever mission was necessary for the sake of freedom. The safety of those souls was also a sacred trust. That much was clear to Tallmadge, and soon he would not only have another chance to see such courage in action but also be a willing player.

During that brutal winter of 1777 and into January 1778, Tallmadge stayed close to General Washington at Valley Forge; in such cramped and miserable quarters, the young officer impressed his commander. He was still somewhat untested and not always as far-sighted as more seasoned officers, but it was clear that both his input and his unsinkable enthusiasm were valued by both subordinates and superiors.

When Washington tapped him to act as spymaster on Long Island, Tallmadge acted quickly. He knew right away whom he would approach to be his man on the ground.

CHAPTER 4

Crossing the Sound

G rowing up, Abraham Woodhull had been a neighbor of Tallmadge's, and he shared many of the young officer's ideals, but that's where their resemblance ended. By all accounts, Woodhull was no bright-eyed, optimistic, jolly-young-man-turned-soldier who ran eagerly into the welcoming arms of the American cause. His sentiments lay with liberty, but as a confirmed bachelor and self-proclaimed old man before the age of thirty, he put such a premium on personal autonomy that he avoided official military service, where he would have been subject to the orders of superiors.

Abraham was his parents' third son, raised under the shadow of a prominent and celebrated family (which included the ill-fated General Nathan Wood-hull, a cousin) to be neither the heir nor the spare to the paternal estate. While his older brothers, Richard V and Adam, were groomed to step into the role of American gentlemen, young Abraham was released to

the freedom of the outdoors. It was a dismissal he neither minded nor resented, as he found the tedium of
schoolwork uninspiring. While his brothers were la-
boring over passages of classical rhetoric, Abraham
gained an intimate knowledge of the landscape of
Long Island, connecting every topographical feature
with its owner.

The Woodhull girls, Susannah and Mary, doted on
their baby brother, and Abraham was equally fond of
them. When Mary married Amos Underhill and moved
with him to Manhattan, Abraham made a habit of visiting them. Sometimes he traversed Long Island and
then crossed the East River to Manhattan, and other
times he caught a ride with a longshoreman rowing
across Long Island Sound to Connecticut and then
traveled southward to the city. He enjoyed these trips,
but the family was soon to face difficult times. In 1768,
at the age of twenty-one, Adam died; six years later, at
the age of thirty, Richard V died. And so, in 1774,
Abraham found himself suddenly and unexpectedly in
position to inherit the Woodhull family's homestead.

It was a windfall he had neither hoped for when it
was out of reach nor relished now that it was his. He
had never considered himself cut from the same fabric
as the rest of the prominent landowners, and had gone
to some pains to distinguish himself from their upright
and uptight behavior. Abraham Woodhull was proud
of being the black sheep of his straitlaced family, and
he assumed the burden of familial duty with reluctance; it smacked of Old World thinking. If he was to
reject King George's authority on the basis that the

monarch had simply been born into his position, why could he not also reject his own family's expectations for him to pick up the mantle of Woodhull respectability simply because he was the sole surviving son-of-a-son-of-a-son-of-a-son-of-a-son?

OCCUPIED NEW YORK

When war erupted the following year, Woodhull's journeys to Manhattan by both the northern and the southern routes became more perilous, though he continued to visit his sister whenever he could. By 1777, New York had fallen from quite a height of Patriotic fervor. Manhattan and its surrounding areas had always leaned Loyalist, but in the early years of the conflict, there was still a significant Patriot population. When the newly penned Declaration of Independence was read publicly the summer before, the reaction had been wildly enthusiastic. Rowdy Patriots tore down a statue of King George in spontaneous protest and melted its four thousand pounds of lead for bullets. General George Washington, while appreciating the mettle (and resourcefulness) demonstrated, chastised some of his own officers involved in what he viewed as an undignified and disrespectful act.

After the British proved victorious at the Battle of Brooklyn and then with the fall of Manhattan, in August and September of 1776, respectively, there was a demographic shift as many Patriots left the city for more like-minded locales and Loyalists flooded into the city that was viewed as a safe haven for those who sided with the Crown. The fire that raged through a significant portion of the city following the Americans' retreat also contributed to the change in population. More than one Patriot lost his home or business to the fire. It might have been worth staying and rebuilding had the conquering army been a sympathetic one, but the loss of shelter, livelihood, *and* political power was too much for many people to bear all at once.

What destruction and politics didn't drive out, filth did. Nicholas Cresswell, an Englishman visiting New York, recorded his disgust with the state of the city following the winter thaw in the spring of 1777. He complained about the sheer number of people crowded into the city's confines, "almost like herrings in a barrel, most of them very dirty and not a small number sick of some disease, the Itch, Pox, Fever, or Flux." He further opined, "If any author had an inclination to write a treatise upon stinks and ill smells, he never could meet with more subject matter than in New York."

For those well-to-do Loyalists who stayed in the city because it was their home, the general squalor was of little concern; there was still a sparkling social scene full of dinner parties and balls, providing a glittering mask of denial. After all, such was urban life, and New York was certainly large enough to absorb whatever elements came its way. The British officers stationed there enjoyed the high life, only occasionally interrupted by the necessary evil of having to earn their pay by leading troops into battle. When the tents were struck and the cannon smoke cleared, they went back to living it up in the ballrooms, coffeehouses, and taverns of Manhattan.

The common foot soldiers stationed there were hardly enjoying the same privileges as their commissioned leadership, but they, too, had the benefits of steady pay and the automatic authority conferred by their uniforms. Life for civilians who were less well-off was harder, as they competed for what resources were left over after the troops were supplied.

For those Patriots who remained behind when the American troops withdrew, life became a kind of fragile maze; it could be successfully navigated if one trod carefully, but a wrong turn or false move could leave one isolated and alone, and a single errant step could cause an irreparable crack. The physical fighting between armies had subsided, but that did not mean peace had filled the vacuum.

Yet despite the disease, stink, vice, and every other undesirable trait with which the city was plagued, New York was still the most desirable piece of real estate on the North American continent. As the geographical heart of the English eastern seaboard, it was strategically significant from both a naval and an economic perspective. And it was still solidly outside of General Washington's grasp—but not out of reach of Abraham Woodhull. Whether or not he was transporting goods back and forth between Manhattan and Long Island without official British sanction was, by his own estimation, no one's business but his own. After all, it was *his* neck on the line if he was caught.

SMUGGLING

Woodhull was infinitely practical and took pride in his pragmatism. What use did a farmer have for frivolity? Unlike a merchant, whose profitability hinged on the art of accurately reading and predicting the social whims of the spending public, a farmer depended on the hard science of nature for his livelihood. But sometimes those worlds intersected—a farmer with a shrewd business sense could capitalize on the tastes and trends of the general population by trading his produce for luxury goods that he could sell for a hefty profit while never having to indulge in the trappings of fashionability himself. What could be more practical than that?

Urbane, bustling New York imported exotic and high-end merchandise from around the globe; such trade was the basis of much of its economy. But its cobblestone streets and tightly packed homes and businesses left little earth for gardens, let alone large-scale farming. And yet the population needed to eat. North of the city, working farms dotted the Hudson Valley, but those areas were largely in Patriot hands. British soldiers closely monitored every road in and out of Manhattan, and farmers who brought in wagons of meats, grains, cheeses, and vegetables for sale in the city were likely to face taxes or even confiscation of part of their goods. Still, it was good business, even if some losses had to be factored in as part of the game.

The farmers and fishermen on Long Island devised ways to get around the British taxes. Some took the ferry that ran between Brooklyn and Manhattan, carrying bundles of food disguised as ordinary goods of little interest to the authorities; others found their own means of transport. One or two men could cross the Sound due west to largely Patriot Connecticut, then travel by foot or else row south to Manhattan with a well-stocked whaleboat. After quickly and easily unloading their goods at high prices to city residents hungry for fresh, wholesome produce, they would fill the skiff up with tea, spices, foreign wines, and trinkets not available on Long Island that they could buy cheaply in the city. Some of these capitalists traded for their own gratification (or that of their families); others, like Woodhull, found they could sell the goods at exaggerated prices to the isolated and luxury-starved residents of Long Island. It was a simple case of supply and demand. Luxury goods were wanted and Woodhull was happy to supply them—in return for silver.

But it was also risky business. The Sound was patrolled by the formidable British navy and, even though smuggling was accepted as common practice, an example was sometimes made of violators. Men who were caught could face anything from a stern warning to a heavy fine to imprisonment. Those who were not caught could expect to live rather comfortably.

Woodhull found himself favoring the lower-risk route of the Brooklyn ferry as he once again began making his regular trips from his home in Setauket to visit his sister Mary and her husband, Amos Underhill, at their Manhattan boardinghouse. This family connection gave him a warm meal and a roof over his head for the night, possibly a built-in clientele (if not among boarders then among neighbors) for his smuggled goods, and, most important, a plausible reason to be headed for the city with regularity. New York was not in a state of siege, and private citizens could travel with some degree of freedom, but regulations were certainly tightened and the occupying army was always on the lookout for suspicious activity that might belie smuggling or even espionage. Of the former, Woodhull was certainly guilty; he had little thought of the latter yet.

Woodhull held his political cards close to the vest; he knew what happened to the families of outspoken dissenters. Even if he chafed under a sense of inherited obligation, he still felt the weight of responsibility to care for his aging parents and his sister Susannah. He quickly squelched any burgeoning sense of Patriotic duty that tried to take root in his mind or in his heart. He couldn't leave to join the army, even if his personality had been better suited for military service. Not with both of his brothers now dead.

No, his place was in Setauket, even if it meant having to endure the inconvenience of the redcoats' watchful eyes on all trade and commerce.

ISLAND LIFE

While New Yorkers were facing their own uncertain future, their friends and relations across the Sound were finding their lives even more disrupted. The soaring population, crime, and demand on resources may not have been anything new to Manhattan residents, but for Long Islanders, it was quite a change from their idyllic existence prior to the war.

In the second half of the eighteenth century, Long Island was still largely rural and wooded, with the town green in front of the church often the only open area for acres in any direction, save for a few cleared patches for crops and pasturelands. Even the shorelines were dense with trees. Combined with the rugged topography of the land itself, that meant sweeping vistas of the sea were not nearly as common as boggy inlets that overlooked more forests or were situated at the foot of small, hilly farms. Fresh produce, meats, cheese, milk, and eggs from these small estates all fetched high prices in the city, though the trade was tightly regulated by the British.

The farmers were supposed to be fairly compensated for whatever goods were procured for the occupying soldiers, but this was not always the case. Instead of cash, locals were often given promissory notes that later proved worthless; sometimes boisterous troops simply helped themselves to a farmer's livestock or orchard, or to a tavern keeper's ale. Even more concerning was the wanton disregard for land rights. The British disassembled fences and barns for the sake of lumber, which cost the owner time and money for repair and replacement and also threatened the future viability of the farm by allowing animals to get loose or exposing plowing equipment to the elements. If the landowner objected to being so grossly misused by the British, he was told to take his complaints to the officer in charge. Disciplinary measures and restitution were never guaranteed—consequences varied according to the moral character of the presiding officer.

All around the British-occupied areas of New York and New Jersey, reports of attacks upon local women by both individual soldiers and groups of the garrisoned troops were made with startling regularity as early as the summer of 1776. Many cases were handled with a casual nonchalance as simply part of the collateral damage of war. On August 5, 1776, Lord Rawdon, a cavalry officer stationed on Staten Island, wrote a rather cavalier letter to his good friend Francis Hastings, tenth Earl of Huntingdon, back home in England, in which Rawdon declared:

> *The fair nymphs of this isle are in wonderful tribulation, as the fresh meat our men have got here has made them as riotous as satyrs. A girl cannot step into the bushes to pluck a rose without running the most imminent risk of being ravished, and they are so little accustomed to these vigorous methods that they don't bear them with the proper resignation, and of consequence we have most entertaining courtsmartial every day.*

In the city, there was already a growing industry catering to the carnal urges of the occupying troops. As Woodhull's sister Mary surely discovered, running a reputable boardinghouse in Manhattan was a growing challenge as the demand grew for rooms that offered more than just a cot, a basin for washing, and a hot meal. But on the more provincial Staten Island and on Long Island there were not nearly as many opportunities for paid pleasure—so women found themselves afraid for their safety even as upper- and middle-class families were often required to open their houses for quartering soldiers. With many men away fighting on either side, or being held as political prisoners, wives and daughters left behind to tend to a house full of strange men with muskets found themselves in a precarious situation. Even if most officers conducted themselves as befitted an English gentleman, there was a nervous tension, a constant fear and distrust that settled over each town where the king's men made themselves at home.

Woodhull had noticed it in the eyes of the men and women he passed on the street each day—that fear and weariness of a war that was still relatively young. Many islanders expressed little or no opinion as they went about their daily lives, but there were some who seemed to speak to one another through glances:

"Did we not welcome the king's army like loyal subjects? Is this how we are to be repaid?"

"Must we go without so they can live in abundance?"

"They attack our farms and our daughters, and yet we are forced to keep silent or be branded a traitor."

"I am subject to King George with my land, my money, and my fidelity but—by God!—I am not subject to his men and certainly not under my own roof!"

AN INTERVIEW

How exactly Tallmadge and Woodhull reconnected and concocted the first phase of their plan is not exactly clear. It is almost certain that Tallmadge intercepted his old neighbor and family friend in Connecticut, as the risk of setting foot in occupied New York City or Long Island would have been too great. Most of Connecticut was still solidly in American hands in August 1778, providing a good meeting point for the two men.

Under heavy cover, whether at a local watering hole or within the home of a well-vetted government official with proven allegiances, Tallmadge informed Woodhull of his charge from Washington. He was to install a ring of spies to convey information from Manhattan either directly over the border to Connecticut or, perhaps more safely, across the Sound to Long Island and from there to the more rural areas of Connecticut—and thus much farther from British inspectors who might possibly intercept the intelligence. There, Tallmadge could receive and analyze the sensitive information before spiriting it away to wherever Washington happened to be encamped at the time, which was almost always within just a few days' ride of New York City.

"You're saying I'd have license to work as I see fit—hire the men I want and carry out . . . the business the way I think it ought to go?" Woodhull asked gruffly.

"Completely," Tallmadge assured him. "General Washington wants the work carried out by men who know the land, the water, and the people—a local man, in other words."

"Who else knows about this? I don't want my name and my business put out there to anyone I don't know and trust."

"Everything would be guarded with the utmost confidence," Tallmadge promised. "Only General Washington and I need know about your involvement." Woodhull seemed twitchy, nervous—and not without cause. Tallmadge therefore felt there was no need to mention Brigadier General Scott, the spymaster for the Continental Army and a man with whom Tallmadge rarely saw eye-to-eye, as his hope was to bypass Scott as much as possible anyway.

Woodhull turned the proposition over carefully in his mind. "But why me, of all the folks on Long Island you could have chosen? What are you to do if I decline your offer?"

Tallmadge looked Woodhull in the eye. "You have a good estate with a good farm and a good income. Now, I know your sister Susannah is still living at home, but there are no wife and no children waiting at home for you whose welfare may cause you to check your daring. You know the countryside, the best places to pick up gossip, which roads to use. I've been away some years but you've stayed on at home, building a life and building relationships. I know things have been difficult since the British landed and I don't envy what you have had to endure watching the redcoats loot and burn the places you love most. You know

(God forbid!) the escape routes. But, most important, I know that no matter what mask you may wear in public right now, you believe that this war must be won for the sake of human dignity. And New York must be had if that is to happen."

There was a moment of silence before Woodhull spoke. "But it's not just me. What about the others you want me to enlist? What makes you think they can be relied upon to carry out their jobs? To stay silent rather than panic the first time a lobsterback comes too near?"

"I assume you would recruit only men you knew to be of stalwart disposition and courage commensurate to the task."

"So I must ask my closest friends to gamble their own fortunes and lives?"

"We went over that already and took those concerns into account." Tallmadge leaned forward. "Abraham, we've known each other for a long time. Our families have known each other for a long time. If you believe that"—he paused and checked his words—"those handful of names we've discussed can be trusted with a mission this important in pursuit of a cause so sacred, then so do I. I have the fullest faith in you to dispatch your duty as well as you and your assistants are able."

"And you promise I won't have any dandified officers from Charleston or Boston or God knows where else landing on my sliver of land and trying to tell me about how things should work?" Woodhull insisted.

Tallmadge raised an eyebrow. "Isn't that exactly the sort of thing that started this war in the first place?"

NEW IDENTITIES

A few days later, on the afternoon of August 25, Major Tallmadge met with his commander in chief at his current encampment in White Plains, New York. The aim of this two-man congress was to allow Tallmadge to recount the meeting in Connecticut and assuage Washington's concern on several fronts—whether Woodhull could be trusted, whether he was a skilled enough judge of character to recruit loyal men, and whether his primary aim was patriotism or profit. The other issue of utmost importance was the creation of pseudonyms. The stakes were far too high for Tallmadge and Woodhull to use their real names, especially in any kind of correspondence. In Tallmadge's case, an intercepted letter would make him an even higher-value target should the British learn he was now dabbling in espionage. In Woodhull's case, living in the midst of the enemy, identification meant immediate arrest likely followed by a trip to the gallows.

The general and the major discussed the best approach to the assignment of names—at once specific enough to be clearly and instantly identifiable to the intended recipient, yet not so unusual as to obviously be a fake name nor so common that an innocent individual who happened to bear the same name might be hunted down by the enemy. Thus, Tallmadge was dubbed "John Bolton," a mild and unassuming moniker with a surname that was among the oldest in the colonies. The genesis of Woodhull's name was a little more creative. Charles Scott's initials were inverted as a nod to his position as chief spymaster for the Continental Army, and Tallmadge selected "Samuel" for a first name, probably in honor of his younger brother, Samuel Tallmadge, who had done some courier work for Patriot efforts on Long Island. The last name, it has been suggested, became an adaptation of "Culpeper," the county in Virginia that bordered the western edge of Washington's boyhood home of Stafford County, and the region in which he did some of his early work as a surveyor. Thus, "Samuel Culper" was born.

Pseudonyms were in place. Courier routes were set. Specifics as to the type of information Washington sought were established. The groundwork was laid for the ring to begin its work. The first two cogs, Tallmadge and Woodhull, were in place to begin turning the wheel that would steadily roll out the defeat of the British in New York. They would not disappear into their new identities and leave their old lives behind. Instead, their spy names would serve as their passports into a double life—Tallmadge as an intelligence officer with a closely guarded secret and a covert post in Connecticut where he would retrieve the latest news, and Woodhull as a man who must go unnoticed in the den while seeking ways to overthrow the lions.

CHAPTER 5

The Ring Springs into Action

Woodhull had his sights set on Caleb Brewster as a fellow spy from the beginning. He had to admire the audacity of the brash longshoreman who was a bull of a man—physically huge and imposing—and was using his intimidating size and tremendous athletic skill to make himself a regular nuisance to the British. Ever the daredevil, he taunted them from his whaler laden with smuggled goods and then amazingly evaded capture. Just as Woodhull knew the landscape, Brewster knew the coves and the waterways, slipping out of reach of the British by ducking into one or another until the patrol gave up trying to catch him red-handed.

But that had always been Brewster's way. Back in June 1775, some local men had circulated a document declaring their determination to fight British oppression, swearing that they would never "become slaves." Despite his usual caution, Woodhull had signed it, as had one of Benjamin Tallmadge's brothers. So, too, had Caleb Brewster. Remembering Brewster's signature and observing the man's high spirits and taste for adventure, Woodhull knew that Brewster would be an easy convert to the mission.

What Woodhull did not know was that Brewster had already embraced the thrill of espionage. The young man had been in correspondence with General Washington since July 1778—several weeks before Tallmadge had recruited Woodhull to manage the ring—reporting on the state of the British warships in New York Harbor, as well as troop movements and naval preparations around Long Island. His reports revealed little new information and were somewhat out-of-date by the time they reached Washington, but the gesture proved to the commander in chief that there were Patriots ready and willing to spy and that a well-organized ring of secret agents could yield real intelligence.

While taking care not to be overheard, Woodhull was probably rather direct in his proposal to Brewster. The man's vigor and fearlessness in openly defying the British navy on the Sound left little doubt about which way his sentiments lay. Already hooked on the adrenaline rush of espionage, Brewster was an easy sell. He enthusiastically agreed to ferry messages to Connecticut and even offered to add his own observations to the reports headed to Tallmadge.

Woodhull supposed that his old friend Austin Roe, however, might prove somewhat more difficult to recruit. Roe was friends with Brewster, and while he was jovial and spirited as well, Roe was also comfortably situated, married, firmly established in his business, and took no joy in evading arrest in a rowboat for sport. But unlike Woodhull, who could find ready buyers for his produce in the city even if he alienated his Loyalist neighbors, or Brewster, who could find work as a longshoreman at any dock that needed the hands, Roe was a tavern keeper. His livelihood was entirely dependent upon the loyal patronage of local folks and the occasional traveler who passed his way and needed a room for the night. Should the spies' work be discovered, they could all expect something far worse than a loss of employment. But suspicions have a way of becoming whispers in small towns, and rumors about Roe's activities could hurt his business even after the war.

Despite initial concerns, Roe was pleased by the mission and eager to offer his service in any way he could. Now a team of three, Woodhull, Brewster, and Roe devised a plan by which their intelligence would make its way across land and water to reach General Washington. Woodhull would operate from Amos Underhill's boardinghouse in Manhattan, a location unlikely to arouse suspicion because of Woodhull's family connection and because he already made fairly regular visits. The information he gathered would leave the city in one of two ways. Either Roe would make the trip into the city on the pretense of purchasing provisions for his business, or else Woodhull himself would travel back to Setauket, where he would leave the papers at Roe's tavern or a predetermined location in a field near Roe's house so the two men would not be seen together. This "dead-drop" method was less likely to raise suspicions but presented a much higher risk of a stranger's stumbling upon the papers before they had been picked up, so the men rarely employed it. The two families were known to be old friends—Roe's father had purchased the building he used for his home and business from the Woodhulls back in 1759—so nothing would seem out of place even if the two men were to be seen together carrying letters for the folks at home or visiting in the city. But Roe and Woodhull took care to ensure that the patterns of their meetings would not become too predictable and seem shady to nosy locals or eagle-eyed British soldiers.

Caleb Brewster, whose family lived just yards away from Roe, would wait for an opportunity to retrieve the papers from Roe. He would then dash across the water when the British navy had their backs turned. On the Connecticut side of the Sound, Tallmadge would be waiting for Brewster to dock and pass off the letters, which Tallmadge would then hand-deliver to the general.

The whole process took approximately two weeks from beginning to end and offered several advantages over the more traditional method of a solitary spy slipping in to gather intelligence and then slipping back out again. Local men were less likely to raise suspicions than an outsider who suddenly appeared in the town, skulked about for a few days, and then disappeared again. Using existing routines also allowed for a longer-term observance that could note changes in patterns and procedures of the troops. And, of course, if one man attracted suspicion, the seemingly convoluted method of passing off information from one member to another would make it much more difficult for the enemy to intercept sensitive documents. The intervening step of entrusting the papers to Roe was a brilliant one. It minimized the connection between Woodhull's frequent trips to and extended stays in the city and Brewster's regular dashes across the water and allowed the men to avoid apparent contact. But the proximity of Brewster's home to Roe's made their familiarity far more natural.

Even as the Culper Ring took shape, Tallmadge's superior, Brigadier General Scott, still clung to the more conventional methods of dispatching spies. He had sent at least five men on separate scouting missions to Long Island, hoping to check their reports against one another for accuracy. He believed that even if one man was caught the others would not be compromised because each mission was conducted independently of the others. What Scott had failed to plan for was the capture of three of his five spies when their presence and suspicious behavior tipped off the British that all was not as it seemed.

Washington preferred this traditional approach at first, but it soon became clear that Scott's method cost lives, and Washington's conscience would not allow him to keep paying that high price. Battles demanded sacrifice, but Washington could not stand to see any more spies go the way of Nathan Hale—and all for nothing. Soon after his Long Island spies were caught,

Scott took a furlough and returned home to Virginia to sort out some personal business. Washington appointed Tallmadge as his replacement. At the tender age of twenty-four, Benjamin Tallmadge became the chief of intelligence, the role that would define his career and ultimately help secure the nascent country's future.

REPORTS BEGIN

Almost immediately, Woodhull revealed himself to be a remarkably acute observer, as well as an extremely nervous operative. On November 23, 1778, Woodhull as Culper wrote to General Washington with a precise count of troops at various towns on Long Island, as well as a request for reimbursement for his expenses: "My business is expensive; so dangerous traveling that I am obliged to give my assistants high wages, but am as sparing as possible."

Washington was impressed with the detailed information he received and spoke with Tallmadge about arranging a face-to-face meeting with his brave new ringleader—a suggestion that rattled Woodhull no small amount. He thought he had made it abundantly clear to Tallmadge that he did not want his association with spying activities to be openly acknowledged in any public way. Of course, the general knew about the ring, but Woodhull felt that his personal appearance before Washington was unnecessary and would raise questions. Because he rarely traveled beyond the city, his neighbors might ask uncomfortable questions. Local friends or relatives in Washington's camp might look askance at his presence there. Besides these objections, it is also likely that Woodhull resisted out of a sense of inferiority; later letters contain apologies for his simple and unschooled writing and his lack of a private fortune with which to bankroll the work. Even though his family held a sizable farm, they were land rich and cash poor, and Woodhull had received a practical education on growing sustainable crops rather than a classical one. Thus, a meeting with an esteemed "gentleman farmer," an archetypal figure of both British and American mythology and of whom Washington was the ideal, would only highlight Woodhull's own shortcomings of learning, culture, and person.

The proposed meeting was abandoned, but Woodhull's hackles remained raised. The more he thought about it, the more he became unnerved by the whole matter—and this agitation was not improved by a slight adjustment made to the delivery route just five weeks later, in January 1779. Instead of Tallmadge personally delivering the letters to General Washington's hand, he was now going to pass them off to General Israel Putnam, who would then carry them and other dispatches from Danbury, Connecticut, to the commander in chief. Even though Putnam, a hero of Bunker Hill, knew nothing of the true identity of "Culper" it was nerve-racking for Woodhull, who feared any involvement of strangers.

Austin Roe also made a move that rankled Woodhull even further; he hired a young man named Jonas Hawkins as an occasional courier, both to dilute suspicion and to get letters into Tallmadge's hands more quickly, because Hawkins could carry information at times when Roe's business prevented him from traveling. Even if Hawkins was not privy to the full extent of the operation, another person now knew at least part of the secret, and this worried Woodhull. But the changes nearly halved the amount of time it took for Woodhull's intelligence to reach Washington, from two weeks to only one. Woodhull couldn't argue against the improvement.

Despite his fraying nerves, Woodhull persisted with his meticulous scouting reports on Manhattan, detailing where British troops were situated and how strong their positions were. He also added a note of personal concern for the rapidly deteriorating state of affairs on Long Island. "I cannot bear the thoughts of the war continuing another year, as could wish to see an end of this great distress. Were I to undertake to give an account of the sad destruction that the enemy makes within these lines I should fail. They have no regard to age, sex, whig or tory," he lamented.

Caleb Brewster supplemented the reports with his own reporting on shipbuilding activities and the particular ships in each Long Island inlet and harbor. "I have returned from the Island this day," Brewster wrote:

> Genl. Erskine [quartermaster general of the British army] remains yet at Southampton. He has been reinforced to the number of 2500. They have three redoubts at South and East Hampton and are heaving up works at Canoe

Place at a narrow pass before you get into
South Hampton. They are building a number
of flat bottom boats. There went a number of
carpenters down last week to South Hampton.
It is thought by the inhabitants that they will
cross over to New London after the Continen-
tal Frigates. Col. Hewlet [of the Third Battal-
ion, DeLancey's brigade] remains yet on
Lloyd's Neck with 350, wood cutters included.
Col. Simcoe [of the Queen's Raiders] remains
at Oyster bay with 300 Foot and Light Horse.
There is no troops from Oyster Bay till you
come to Jamaica. There is one Regt. of High-
landers and some at Flushing and Newtown,
the numbers I cannot tell, but not a regiment
at both places.

Together, these reports began to create a rich and
detailed picture of New York's defenses, as well as provide important clues about the enemy's future strategy.

A SECRET WEAPON

As the spring of 1779 crept into New York, Woodhull
was near panic, obsessed with the fear that he was on
the verge of being found out and arrested. He was certain that the British were suspicious of his frequent
trips to Manhattan, perhaps even shadowing him to
learn his whereabouts and activities in the city, and
noting any patterns of behavior following his return
from each trip. There was one promising development,

however, which gave Woodhull a sense of relief: the long-awaited arrival of a particular concoction intended to give him an added layer of security. Washington had obtained a supply of invisible ink and issued Woodhull a vial of the precious substance for the writing of the Culper reports.

The practice of writing with disappearing inks was nothing new. For centuries people had been communicating surreptitiously through natural and chemically manipulated inks that became visible when exposed to heat, light, or acid. A message written in onion juice, for example, dried on paper without a trace but became readable when held to a candle. Secret correspondence in the British military often had a subtle *F* or *A* in the corner indicating to the recipient whether the paper should be exposed to fire or acid to reveal its message.

But the usefulness of these devices was limited because they were all so well known. Washington wanted something innovative and unknown to the British, and he received just such a solution from none other than John Jay, the statesman and spymaster of the Hudson Valley.

Sir James Jay, John Jay's older brother, had traveled to England in 1762 in an effort to raise funds for King's College in New York. In 1763, he was knighted by King George and remained in England for a time before returning to America just as hostilities were heating up between the colonists and the mother country. Though his political views would shift during the war, Sir James initially sided with the Patriots and used his knowledge of chemistry to develop an ink that became visible only through the application of a specific "sympathetic stain." Both the ink and the reagent required a complicated recipe and special workshop, making them valuable commodities that were also extremely difficult to manufacture in any great quantity. The younger Jay brother took it upon himself to learn the painstaking process so he could personally make them for General Washington's use.

When Washington received his first batch of the ink, he was delighted with the effect. It was, in a way, an unbreakable code, impervious to any of the usual means of discovery. Even if the British suspected a white-ink message in any particular letter, they had no way of revealing it unless they, too, were in possession of the related formula. Because the recipe was Jay's unique creation, it was nearly impossible for them to decipher these dispatches.

That small vial of ink must have seemed like the Holy Grail to the increasingly nervous Woodhull—a precious chalice that held a mystical liquid that could save his life. He had been waiting for its arrival for months, ever since the ink's existence was first mentioned to him, aware of how sparing he must be with its use and yet eager to entrust all of his gathered reports to its protection. He would never fully relax as long as he was living a double life, that much was clear, but he did find great comfort in possessing that ink. He could hardly wait to get started writing back to Washington all that he was witnessing as New York began to thaw from another long winter.

A CRISIS POINT

Just a few days before receiving the long-awaited white ink, Woodhull had composed a letter on April 10, 1779, that reveals something of the concern he was feeling for the security of his missive. "*Sir.* No. 10," the letter begins, using a crude code to disguise the name of the intended recipient. Immediately, he launched into an apology, stating:

> *Whenever I sit down I always feel and know my Inability to write a good Letter. As my calling in life never required it—Nor led to consider how necessary a qualification it was for a man—and much less did I think it would ever fall to my lot to serve in such publick and important business as this, and my letters perused by one of the worthiest men on earth. But I trust he will overlook any imperfections he may discover in the dress of my words, and rest assured that I indevour to collect and covey the most accurate and explicit intelligence that I possibly can; and hope it may be of some service toward alleviating the misery of our distressed Country, nothing but that could have induced me to undertake it.*

It was clear to all involved that Woodhull was suffering from severely strained nerves and might soon quit the whole business were he not reassured as to the value of his information and the confidence the other members of the ring had in his ability to obtain it in total security. Tallmadge therefore undertook a dangerous trip with Brewster back across Long Island Sound to Woodhull's home in Setauket in order to offer him this support in person, as well as to give him payment for his expenses and pains. However, as if to underscore the fact that Woodhull's fears were rooted in reality rather than paranoia, several British officers unexpectedly took up quarter in Woodhull's home at that same time, forcing Tallmadge to keep cover and only see his friend briefly before returning to Connecticut.

It was a perfect storm of worry for Woodhull: One of the most wanted men in the Continental Army had shown up on his land even as there were British troops making themselves at home under his roof. One or the other would have been quite enough to push him to the brink of nervous exhaustion; the two occurring simultaneously was sufficient to tip him over the edge.

One evening, Woodhull sat at his writing desk, composing a letter to Washington from his small supply of invisible ink, acutely aware of the presence of British soldiers in the neighboring chamber. Glancing repeatedly at the door as he hurried to finish his report, he sat ready to cover his work and divert attention should he be interrupted. The old house was quiet, which was a comfort and allowed him to breathe a little easier than he might have otherwise.

Suddenly, the door flew open and two figures barged into the room. Woodhull leapt up, attempting to sweep all his papers to his chest in the process, and overturned the table. It fell to the ground with a crash, scattering its contents and smashing the vial of ink upon the wooden floor. But where Woodhull expected to hear the roar of discovery from a British officer, he instead heard the giggles of teenage girls. Two cousins, who had observed the twitchy depression from which Woodhull was suffering, had taken it into their heads to surprise him in such a manner as to make him laugh. The joke had the opposite effect. "Such an excessive fright and so great a turbulence of passions so wrought on poor Culper that he has hardly been in tolerable health since," Tallmadge wrote to Washington, recounting the event as Woodhull had told it to him. Woodhull apparently managed to salvage some of the ink, since his next letter to the general was composed in the stain, but his supply was severely compromised, as was what little peace of mind he had remaining.

Things only continued to worsen for Woodhull. Just a few days later, while in Huntington (about twenty miles away), he was held up by highwaymen who took all the money he was carrying but were unaware that he was in possession of papers that would have proved even more valuable if turned over to the British. Woodhull, according to Tallmadge, "was glad to escape with his life." It had been a coincidence, with Woodhull simply another random victim of the crime wave that had seemingly taken over Long Island, but what happened next was no coincidence at all. His worst fears were confirmed: Woodhull had become a target.

MANHUNT

John Wolsey was just one of many privateers operating in Long Island Sound. Privateers made their living through a combination of smuggling and theft on the water. Akin to piracy in many ways, privateering was a popular profession at the time for residents on both sides of the Sound. That spring, Wolsey, a Connecticut man who made the trip to and from Long Island quite regularly, found himself in British custody. Fearing for his life, he was desperate to secure leniency.

How he happened to know anything about the doings of Abraham Woodhull is unclear. Perhaps someone at Roe's tavern had caught on to the scheme and spoke a little too freely when ale loosened his tongue. Perhaps Wolsey noticed that Woodhull traveled to see his sister in Manhattan more often than fraternal duty might otherwise call for, and that Caleb Brewster seemed always to be passing by Wolsey's own boat on urgent business a day or two after Woodhull's return. Whatever the case, Wolsey named Woodhull as a person of interest, and his betrayal seemed a credible enough threat to rouse Lieutenant Colonel John Simcoe, a British cavalry officer, from his comfortable lodging in Oyster Bay and to send him over the nearly fifty miles of road eastward to Setauket. With a handful of the Queen's Rangers in tow, Simcoe intended to arrest Woodhull on suspicion of espionage.

Simcoe's men surrounded the Woodhull house, muskets poised and sabers at their sides, and Simcoe pounded on the door, demanding that Woodhull be handed over. Richard, Abraham's elderly father who had already lost his two older sons to untimely deaths, must have felt an overwhelming sense of relief that he could report honestly that Abraham was away in the city and not at home. The soldiers searched the house and interrogated the family, but it was quickly evident that the old man had been telling the truth. This was not the outcome Simcoe had desired—he knew that Woodhull would catch wind of his presence before he arrived home and would dispose of any incriminating evidence. Furious that the opportunity to catch a suspected spy red-handed had been squandered, Simcoe ordered the suspect's father beaten in his stead. The rangers fell upon Richard, bludgeoning him while the rest of the family looked on in horror. Once the old man lay crumpled on the ground, the troops rode off. Simcoe was confident that Abraham, upon his return, would interpret the message loud and clear: "This is what happens to the families of spies."

The attack came as a shock to Woodhull. It was terrible to watch his father struggle feebly to recover from the attack even as the summer came on quickly and the heat and flies only seemed to intensify his suffering. Abraham Woodhull realized that though his absence had saved his life, he could no longer afford the suspicion brought on by his frequent trips to New York, and said as much to Tallmadge, who was forced to explain to General Washington what his spies were enduring back home. Washington heard the story with compassion, and wrote back to Tallmadge promising "more of the liquid Culper writes for" and assuring him that "should suspicions of him rise so high as to render it unsafe to continue in New York I should wish him by all means to employ some person of whose attachments and abilities he entertains the best opinion, to act in his place." Woodhull eagerly took him up on that offer.

Meanwhile, back in his cozy quarters in Oyster Bay, Colonel Simcoe had little notion of the tangled web he'd woven—that the man he'd tried in vain to arrest was, at that same moment, recruiting to his cause another man who already also deeply hated Simcoe for his own personal reasons.

CHAPTER 6

Townsend Joins the Fight

Espionage was, by no means, a gentleman's game in the eighteenth century. In a world ruled by honor, a career of deception and duplicity carried little of the allure and intrigue that it would come to enjoy among later generations. Spies were everywhere, but the general rule was that one gathered intelligence for the sake of bragging rights later on, for the money it paid out now, for the glamorous life brought by proximity to those in power, or for sheer ideological fanaticism.

Mild-mannered, bookish Robert Townsend fit none of those molds. He was no braggart, had no sumptuous tastes or mercenary tendencies, and while he harbored certain tightly held beliefs, he was no zealot. He was a quiet boy from a prominent Long Island family with a history of independent thinking that he had inherited. A peaceable man, he did his best to stay out of the war—until an event forced him to take a stand.

THE TOWNSENDS OF OYSTER BAY

Like their Setauket neighbors, the Tallmadges and the Woodhulls, the Townsends were a proud and ancient family by American standards. The fourth generation of Townsends born in America included Samuel Townsend, an outspoken and intrepid man who in 1738, at the age of twenty-one, had purchased six acres of land in the heart of Oyster Bay, near to the water and on the road to the mill. The property, which he christened the Homestead, included a small house of practical design: two rooms built atop two other rooms, with a central chimney to distribute heat throughout. Over the next several years, Samuel hired local builders to expand the structure to a total of eight rooms in the saltbox style. When the renovation and expansion were complete, he moved in, opened a general store, and married a local girl. It was at the Homestead that he and his wife, Sarah, began to cultivate both a fairly sizable orchard as well as a sizable family. There were eight children in that fifth generation of Townsends: four sons, a daughter, another son, and two more daughters. Samuel also acquired a fleet of four ships that traversed the Atlantic—east, north, and south—which, in turn, kept his shop well stocked and allowed him to trade in just about anything from fabric to rum, molasses, spices, sugar, and snuff.

Besides his small fleet and well-provisioned shop, which was the most prominent in Oyster Bay, Samuel was also well known for his political views, which were often at odds with those in power. In 1758, about halfway through the French and Indian War, he had fired off a strongly worded letter to the New York General Assembly on the subject of the treatment of prisoners. Townsend found fault with the way enemy combatants were being sheltered and provided for by the colonial arm of the British Crown and wasted no words informing the assemblymen of such. He was arrested and brought before the assembly to justify his conduct of insulting them so openly. Several days under lock and key and a stiff fine left him promising no further outbursts—a promise that lasted for a while. As the local schoolmaster noted in his journal, in the weeks following, Samuel "has been as still as a mouse in a cheese."

He took on the role of town clerk and when talk of independence began to circulate, Samuel was generally considered one of those who favored a break with the Crown, even though he seemed to consider himself middle of the road on the issue. His stances and politicking gradually got the better of him and again landed him in hot water with the local authorities more than once. His children, in the meantime, were growing into successful adults, their business connections largely unsullied by their father's reputation as a rabble-rouser and a Patriot.

ODD MAN OUT

Solomon Townsend was, by all accounts, the consummate oldest son. He was just as eager a merchant as his father and, after a short apprenticeship, assumed the captaincy of one of his father's ships. After proving himself for several years with voyages to Canada, Portugal, and the Azores, he took over a European trading route on a three-rigged ship for the Buchanan family, staunch Loyalists related to the Townsends by marriage.

The second son, Samuel Junior, began working in North Carolina as part of the flax trade, but died in 1773 at the age of twenty-three or twenty-four. As the third Townsend son, William, was employed elsewhere when Samuel Junior passed away, the fourth son, Robert, went south to briefly take his brother's place before returning to New York.

Born on November 25, 1753, Robert was in many ways out of place in the Townsend family—as dark and lean as Solomon was blond and broad, and as shy and reserved as William (nicknamed the "flower of the family") was gallant and flirtatious. His desire was not for adventure or prestige; of a much more bookish disposition than his father or brothers, he preferred to work quietly behind the scenes, managing the ledgers and accounts and inspecting incoming shipments—anything that kept him out of the limelight and the ribaldry that the other Townsend men shared with their sailors and clients. Not that Robert resented their quick wit and hearty laughter; in fact, he rather admired the spirit the rest of his family brought to life. But as the fourth son was quickly followed by a long-awaited daughter, he had learned almost from infancy that he had no hope of being heard over his clamorous brothers or coddled as his mother's darling, so he separated himself by being the quiet one of such a rowdy bunch.

Old Samuel probably wondered how Robert maintained subdued habits as he watched his young son with his loping gait stride past a rough-and-tumble wrestling match on the family's front lawn. The Townsend family tree was peppered with Quakers, though Samuel had married a daughter of prominent Episcopalians, which, along with his taste for luxury goods and the occasional bit of ostentatious accessorizing, put him largely on the outs with the Friends among his relatives. But Robert seemed to have inherited all the Quaker tendencies of somber dress, quiet habit, and humble bearing that Samuel had rejected, and they suited him well. Robert's nature made him fastidious and gave him an eye for detail—traits essential for success in the merchant trade.

"Still," Samuel thought to himself, "the boy could use a little less rigidity in his life."

There was likely no small source of amusement in the Townsend family when Samuel secured the terms of Robert's apprenticeship in Manhattan with Templeton & Stewart, a merchant house in the unfortunately named "Holy Ground" district, a disreputable part of town. The blocks around Barclay, Church, and Vesey Streets were not more dangerous than any other slum in the city, but they were morally treacherous. The district's proximity to the docks meant it was prime real estate for both profit-conscious merchants who wanted to be near their ships returning from voyages and for ladies of pleasure who wanted to be near randy sailors returning from months at sea.

Surrounded by brothels, whores, and their clientele, straitlaced Robert distinguished himself at his work and navigated the seedy streets without a whiff of scandal about him in what was almost certainly a very lonely time for the young man. He marked the close of his teenage years in the firm's employment, dealing with almost every other commodity than the one being plied in the streets and cathouses around it.

CHOOSING ALLEGIANCES

Robert was not quite twenty-two when the first shots were fired at Lexington and Concord. For all of his differences from the rest of his family, he shared something of his father's Patriotic fervor. The battlefields in Massachusetts seemed far away, though, and many people expected the conflict to resolve itself before formal combat ever crossed the borders of New York State. By the following summer, however, it was clear that such assumptions were wrong. The Declaration of Independence was signed in July, war was moving inevitably closer to home, and all men of fighting age in the mid-Atlantic region were forced to make the difficult decision of whether to enlist—and on what side.

On August 22, 1776, British troops began pouring onto Long Island while the Americans hunkered down in their positions in Manhattan and in the area of Brooklyn, hoping to protect the mainland of New York City. The record of proceedings from the Provincial

Congress for the state of New York show that on Saturday, August 24, 1776, among other motions adopted was the unanimous resolution that "*Robert Townsend* be a Commissary to supply the Brigade with provisions till such time as *Genl Washington* shall give further orders for that purpose." A footnote further identifies the young man named as "Son of *Samuel Townsend,* the member for *Queens* County." According to the following morning's records, Samuel Senior made further recommendations for the purchasing process by which the newly appointed commissary should supply provisions to Brigadier General Nathaniel Woodhull and the Queens County militia.

So began Robert Townsend's whirlwind tenure in the Continental Army. Fighting broke out across Long Island and Manhattan in the early morning hours of the twenty-seventh, just days after Robert's appointment had been confirmed. The Queens County militia, guarding the ill-fated Jamaica Pass, suffered greatly in battle; their beloved Brigadier General Woodhull was mortally wounded. Robert's service did not last much beyond the Battle of Brooklyn, nor did his father's career as a leader for the Patriot cause on Long Island. Samuel was arrested in early September (though he avoided an unpleasant imprisonment when Thomas Buchanan, of the same family for which Solomon was working, vouched for his character). A few days later, on September 10, Samuel was called into court to swear his allegiance to the Crown. He humbly complied and rather meekly returned to the Homestead.

By the end of 1776, nearly thirteen hundred other

men from Queens County had taken that same vow of loyalty, though how many did so under duress is unknowable. Robert followed his father's example and took the distasteful pledge, too. He left Oyster Bay soon afterward and returned to his quiet life as a merchant in Manhattan, running a modest dry goods shop near the Fly Market in lower Manhattan while the city cleaned up from the great fire that had ravaged it following the retreat of the Americans.

New York was now solidly in British hands, but it mattered little to Robert. His unobtrusive personality and lack of any distinguishing battlefield heroics during his brief service were perhaps his greatest allies in allowing him to continue to work and prosper in the midst of the enemy. But every man has a breaking point—a moment when he has seen one atrocity too many, weathered one insult too many, stayed still for one day too long—and he knows he must act or hate himself for keeping silent.

For Robert Townsend, that moment arrived in the fall of 1778. As Abraham Woodhull and his initial ring were beginning their intelligence war against the British in Manhattan and Long Island, the occupying armies were settling in quite comfortably in various private residences including the Homestead, Robert Townsend's beloved home, in Oyster Bay.

Lieutenant Colonel John Simcoe, the man who had ordered the beating of Woodhull's father, decided that the Townsend family's house fit his purposes quite nicely and proceeded to set up his headquarters in the main part of the home, sequestering the family to just a few back rooms and the shop. At Simcoe's orders, British troops destroyed the orchard, of which old Samuel had been so proud, to feed British fires and help build a fort. Wood from all over town, including churches and private structures, was commandeered for this effort in a move that was very much in keeping with Simcoe's reputation as a heartless combatant. The town operated as if under martial law, with roughly 470 enemy soldiers quartering there, including Hessian brute squads that roamed the streets to make sure residents stayed indoors at night. There were public lashings for those who displeased the soldiers and little recourse for those who brought complaints. The town was quickly descending into a simmering chaos, and any lingering Loyalist feelings among the good people of Oyster Bay were rapidly evaporating.

Old Samuel Townsend's history of outspoken political opinions was well known to the whole community and likely the cause of his "special" treatment from the Queen's Rangers. That his house was one of the more comfortably situated and furnished dwellings in the town was a bonus.

When Robert returned home in November 1778 to visit his family, he was no doubt shocked by his father's defeated appearance and posture.

"What has happened to you, Father?" Robert cried upon approaching the house.

Samuel shook his head. There were too many soldiers around to dare voice any dissatisfaction with the current state of things. "I have been given the honor of playing host to His Majesty's troops," he said, somewhat shakily. "Who could have imagined our humble Homestead would be put to such a purpose as this?"

Tales of hardships and abuses, recounted in hushed tones and with sideways glances, seasoned Robert's meals during his time at home. He burned with anger as he learned of the wanton liberties taken with neighbors' properties and lives, but he could only stare in mute fury as he observed how the soldiers, including Colonel Simcoe himself, flirted openly with his sisters under their father's own roof.

At the conclusion of his visit, Robert returned to his shop in Manhattan, but he was haunted by what he had seen. The crime, the squalor—these were the unfortunate accessories of city life. Or so he had assumed. But now he had seen that Oyster Bay and countless other towns that dotted Long Island were not immune to the collateral damage of war. Rumors continued to reach him during the spring of atrocities committed by Simcoe and others against unarmed citizens, including the wounds inflicted upon old Richard Woodhull. But what could anyone do? The Townsend family stood as much of a chance of evicting Simcoe from their property as they did of expelling the whole enemy encampment from Long Island. There was no other option. They were in British-held territory, so British laws stood and protesters fell—or hanged.

The feelings of frustration and helplessness weighed heavily upon Robert. Each day, British soldiers and common New York citizens alike came into his shop to purchase everyday items such as buttons and paper. He knew he would do his family no favors if he took up arms against this army—they would only be labeled as having ties to a belligerent. Besides, Robert was not a fighting man and his previous service had been focused on supply tents, not trenches; his soul was not the sort to be stirred by marching feet keeping time to a fife tune and drumbeat.

Robert admired the way that his older brother Solomon had found his own way to steer his allegiances. Still sailing for the Loyalist Buchanan family, in 1777 Solomon had carried supplies for the British army to Montreal ahead of the invasion of northern New York. But in the spring of 1778, roughly eight months before Simcoe had commandeered the Townsend family home for his own uses, Solomon had made a calculated move. He left his employment with the Buchanans and had managed to visit with none other than Benjamin Franklin in France. Obtaining a letter from Franklin vouching for his patriotism and fidelity to the American cause, Solomon then boarded an American warship and traveled back across the Atlantic to relaunch his career at home, sailing and trading under the protection of the Continental Army and supplying its troops with much-needed provisions. Robert, meanwhile, was left shaken by his visit home later that fall, and felt the weight of inaction as he walked the streets of occupied New York under the British flag and did business with His Majesty's troops for such trifles as ribbons and sugar.

Despite his internal struggles in the months following his return to Manhattan from his trip home to

Oyster Bay, Townsend was almost certainly surprised
and was not easily won over when Woodhull made his
proposal to work as a spy just as a hot, dusty summer
was beginning in 1779. He was debating his own role
in the struggle for independence, that much was true.
But he was not like his brothers, so brashly fearless
and ready for any adventure; he was Robert, the quiet
one (some might even say the timid one) of the
Townsend boys. His was the name all the relations
and neighbors forgot when speaking of his family,
and he was perfectly content that things should stay
that way.

CULPER JUNIOR

It is possible that the notion of spying had already
crossed Robert Townsend's mind before Abraham
Woodhull darkened the door of his shop in the late
spring of 1779. It may have already been clear to
Townsend that he was privy to scraps of conversation
between soldiers in his own shop, to noting the flow of
supplies and men into and out of the harbor as he inspected his own shipments on the docks, to observing
the habits and patterns of the higher-ranking officers
who graced James Rivington's posh new coffeehouse
just down the street. It must have been clear to
Townsend that his position in the city gave him access
to potentially valuable information. But even if such a
fancy had introduced itself to his mind, it does not
mean it was a welcome thought or one that he relished.

And even if he had been eager to undertake such an effort, he would have had no channel for it, no clearly defined plan for how to get such information into the hands of those to whom it meant something—until he found himself across the table from the old acquaintance who offered him a new mission and a new name: Samuel Culper Jr.

"I have disclosed every secret to you and laid before you every instruction that has been handed to me," Woodhull said, leaning back in his chair after the long conversation. "I have told you the whole business."

Townsend looked at his friend skeptically. Despite their nearness in age, they had never been especially close—both geography and temperament had kept them at a distance from each other. But everyone on Long Island, it seemed, was related to everyone else if you went back a generation or two. Townsend knew their families were connected somehow, and they trusted each other because of it. Even more important than blood ties, though, were ideological ones. Townsend understood that Woodhull had a heart for the cause of liberty, despite his gruff exterior; his trust in Townsend, considering him worthy of such an undertaking, was moving.

Townsend looked across the table to where Woodhull watched him, his face eager for a decision. He had laid out the nature of the mission—every risk, fright, and sleepless night it had brought him—in painful detail. Townsend knew that if he agreed to join the silent fight by taking over the observations in Manhattan, it would wear him down as much as it had Woodhull. Though they were different in personality (Woodhull somewhat cantankerous and Townsend merely reserved), Townsend suspected they were quite alike in their desire to simply be left in peace. A double life would only erode whatever sense of calm he had managed to create for himself, but he also suspected that denying a chance to fight back would erode his conscience.

He was frightened—frightened of all the unthinkable possibilities if he were ever found out, frightened that he already knew too much, frightened of what would happen if he sat by and did nothing.

Townsend reached across the table and shook Woodhull's hand. It was not without trepidation, but it was a handshake nonetheless.

The two men talked long into the night, discussing every eventuality, every risk, and every pressing reason why those risks didn't ultimately matter. Woodhull would add a "Senior" to his code name, and Townsend could become "Culper Junior." No one need ever know—nor even have the means to discover—the real man behind the intelligence reports.

Woodhull's earlier desire for anonymity now paled in comparison to Townsend's insistence that no one other than Woodhull and the courier, not even General Washington, should be aware of his involvement. Townsend was leery even of the courier knowing his face but relented on the point out of necessity.

Townsend did not accept the assignment with enthusiasm. However, despite his fear and reluctance, he was also Samuel Townsend's son. Though he might not share his father's fiery boldness, he was no less a man of brave conviction. With that conviction hardened by his father's mistreatment by Simcoe and his men, he was ready to join the ring. Woodhull wrote to Washington on June 20:

> *My success hath exceeded my most sanguine expectations. I have communicated my business to an intimate friend. . . . It was with great difficulty I gained his complyance, checked by fear. He is a person that hath the interest of our Country at heart and of good reputation, character and family as any of my acquaintance. I am under the most solomn obligations never to disclose his name to any but the Post, who unavoidably must know it. I have reason to think his advantages for serving you and abilities are far superior to mine.*

WASHINGTON'S ORDERS

General Washington was delighted with the proposal and, together with Tallmadge, drafted a detailed list of guidelines and directives for his new agent in New York. The full document, included below, offers an intimate perspective on Washington's philosophies regarding spying, and the specific mission of Culper Junior:

INSTRUCTIONS.

C—— Junr, to remain in the City, to collect all the useful information he can—to do this he should mix as much as possible among the officers and Refugees, visit the Coffee Houses, and all public places. He is to pay particular attention to the movements by land and water in and about the city especially. How their transports are secured against attempt to destroy them—whether by armed vessels upon the flanks, or by chains, Booms, or any contrivances to keep off fire Rafts.

The number of men destined for the defence of the City and Environs, endeavoring to designate the particular corps, and where each is posted.

To be particular in describing the place where the works cross the Island in the Rear of the City—how many Redoubts are upon the line from River to River, how many Cannon in each, and of what weight and whether the Redoubts are closed or open next the city.

Whether there are any Works upon the Island of New York between those near the City and the works at Fort Knyphausen or Washington, and if any, whereabouts and of what kind.

To be very particular to find out whether any works are thrown up on Harlem River, near Harlem Town, and whether Horn's Hook is fortifyed. If so, how many men are kept at each place, and what number and what sized Cannon are in those works.

To enquire whether they have dug Pits within and in front of the lines and Works in general, three or four feet deep, in which sharp pointed stakes are fixed. These are intended to receive and wound men who attempt a surprise at night.

The state of the provisions, Forage and Fuel to be attended to, as also the Health and Spirits of the Army, Navy and City.

These are the principal matters to be observed within the Island and about the City of New York. Many more may occur to a person of C—— Junr's penetration which he will note and communicate.

C—— Senior's station to be upon Long Island to receive and transmit the intelligence of C—— Junior.

As it is imagined that the only post of consequence which the enemy will attempt to hold upon Long Island in case of attack will be at Brooklyn, I would recommend that some inhabitant in the neighborhood of that place, and seemingly in the interest of the enemy, should be procured, who might probably gain daily admission into the Garrison by carrying on marketing, and from him intelligence might be gained every day or two of what was passing within, as the strength of the Garrison, the number and size of the Cannon, &c.

*Proper persons to be procured at convenient
distances along the Sound from Brooklyn to Newtown whose business it shall be to observe and report what is passing upon the water, as whether
any Vessels or Boats with troops are moving,
their number and which way they seem bound.*

*There can be scarcely any need of recom-
mending the greatest Caution and secrecy in a
Business so critical and dangerous. The following seem to be the best general rules:*

*To intrust none but the persons fixed upon to
transact the Business.*

*To deliver the dispatches to none upon our
side but those who shall be pitched upon for the
purpose of receiving them and to transmit them
and any intelligence that may be obtained to no
one but the Commander-in-Chief.*

Washington thought Brooklyn was the one place
on Long Island that the British would regard as indispensable. Because the Culper Ring's route of conveying messages passed directly from Manhattan to
Brooklyn, before continuing on to Setauket and across
the Sound to Connecticut, the courier would have an
excellent opportunity to observe military activity in
Brooklyn and could add any relevant information to
the letter he was carrying from Townsend. In short,
the route seemed as close to an ideal arrangement as
Washington could hope for at the time.

SHOPKEEPER AND REPORTER

Robert Townsend's career as a spy began in that summer of 1779. His fears of the courier knowing his identity proved largely needless—Woodhull himself (at least at first) seems to have been the primary person who retrieved Townsend's reports to begin their circuitous route to General Washington. Woodhull's name appears in the ledger of Townsend's store several times during that season: July 18, August 15, and August 31. And they certainly saw each other more often than that. A letter to Tallmadge from Woodhull on July 9 reveals that the pair had recently met, and in a letter to Washington dated July 15, Townsend wrote: "I saw S. C. [Samuel Culper] Senr. a few days ago, and informed him of the arrival of 10 sail of vessels from the West Indies, with Rum, &c. and a small fleet from Halifax, but no Troops."

In fact, Townsend's detailed reports on naval activities were far more precise than any Woodhull had been able to provide, but Townsend's difficulties with obtaining good troop counts for the army reveal how seriously he took his work. "I am sorry that I cannot give you an exact account of the situation of the troops," he penned on August 6:

> *You may think that I have not taken sufficient pains to obtain it. I assure you that I have, and find it more difficult than I expected. It is some measure owing to my not having got into a regular line of getting intelligence. To depend upon*

common reports would not do. I saw and con-
versed with two officers of different corps from
Kings-bridge from neither of whom I could
obtain an account of the situation of the army
there. I was afraid of being too particular.

Townsend needed a way to move more freely about the city, making inquiries and giving people a reason to trust him. In other words, he needed a cover story, and he found one just down the street in the coffeehouse and print shop of an English expatriate named James Rivington. A printer and a bookseller by trade, Rivington had left England in 1760 over some unpleasantness (most likely having to do with losing his share of his father's business in horse racing), sailed to America, and opened up a printing shop first in Philadelphia and then later in New York City. In 1773, he started publishing his own newspaper as a neutral press with the tagline "Open and Uninfluenced," but eventually it began to promote (as did so many newspapers of the era) a very specific and forceful worldview. In Rivington's case, it was loyalty to King George, a stance that got him hung in effigy by the Sons of Liberty and mocked openly in Patriot writings—gestures that seemed to greatly amuse him.

Townsend had always had a knack for writing; for all of his natural reserve in speaking, he could be very expressive with a pen, and his meticulous, detailed-oriented nature that had served him well inspecting cargo ships also lent itself to composing interesting letters. Recognizing a perfect cover opportunity, he applied for a job at Rivington's paper to write the occasional column of local interest. Rivington recognized the quiet shopkeeper from down the street and was happy to take him up on his offer to contribute to the *Royal Gazette*'s offerings.

It was a stroke of brilliance on Townsend's part. He now had the perfect excuse for asking questions, jotting down details, and querying various movements of troops and matériel into, out of, and around the city. What was more, Rivington's Tory politics would help deflect any suspicion that Townsend might be harboring Patriotic sentiments.

Townsend found himself quite busy as he adjusted to the work of three jobs: shopkeeper, journalist, and undercover agent. As a solitary man with no family and few friends to distract him, he may have found the new duties a nerve-racking but interesting distraction. His association with Rivington likely introduced new acquaintances to his circle as well, as the prosperous set flocked to the coffeehouse to be seen in such esteemed company as the British officers. If Townsend's plain, dark clothes set him apart from the fashionable gentlemen and ladies who discussed politics and soirees, military strategy and dinner parties, no one seemed to mind too much.

Townsend might even have caught sight of a familiar face or two among the coffee-sipping patrons. He might have spotted an old acquaintance from Oyster Bay, or the nephew of a neighbor, or a member of a prominent Long Island family such as the Floyds, or perhaps even one of his own distant cousins. There was no reason for him to fear such recognitions, should they occur, however. His shop was situated just a few yards away and had been for several years, so it was completely natural for him to be found at the coffeehouse, making the acquaintance of all who came through.

MAJOR JOHN ANDRÉ

Another, more sinister figure was establishing himself at Rivington's coffeehouse at the same time as Townsend. The British had wasted no time in developing their own counterspy network. In the spring of 1779, General Henry Clinton had appointed the dashing young major John André as his chief intelligence officer. The major had impressed the general with his wit and savvy when the general arrived in Philadelphia in the early months of 1778. Now, a little over a year after they first became acquainted, Clinton entrusted André with the task of managing the espionage efforts in the colonies, with a specific eye on New York. André and Clinton were well aware that Washington was desperate to retake New York and had to be sending spies there. Eager to intercept Patriot agents, the new intelligence officer set up his headquarters in Manhattan.

André was one of those individuals who thrive wherever planted. He'd always been a rather worldly man; his father was from Geneva and his mother from Paris, and they had raised him in London, educating him with high hopes for a future in diplomacy. He was fluent in several languages, including English, French, German, and Italian, was a gifted artist, and often composed comical verses much to the amusement of his comrades. He was also famed as a party planner and a social coordinator, having directed and painted many of the sets for a celebratory theatrical event in honor of General Howe's return to England from Philadelphia. He had been the toast of that city during the occupation, and was rumored to have offered more than just brotherly love to several ladies therein. Among those who were thought to have fancied him was Peggy Shippen, a sparkling teenager from a prominent Loyalist family, who was renowned as much for her graciousness as for her beauty.

By the summer of 1779, André had moved on to New York and Shippen had recently married a widower named Benedict Arnold, a general in the Continental Army who had gotten to know her when the Americans reclaimed the city the previous year. It was an unlikely alliance given Arnold's employment and her family's politics, but one that seemed to delight bride and groom alike. André, for his part, considered New York a step up from Philadelphia, as it was the closest thing America had to offer, in terms of bustle and variety, to his hometown of London. He quickly became a fixture on the social scene, charming all company with his gallant manners and jovial personality, and spending many languid afternoons sipping coffee and trading ideas at Rivington's shop.

André found yet another advantage to his patronage of Rivington's establishment: He now had a willing publisher for his poems. Rivington was happy to publish any doggerel the dashing young Major André sent his way, as even the silly rhymes of such a popular figure were sure to sell papers among the Loyalist set in

Manhattan. So it was that the counterspy unwittingly published his poetry next to the columns of his biggest target.

THE LADY

It was probably through his newspaper work that Townsend first made the acquaintance of a young female socialite, of whom he informed Woodhull. In his letter dated August 15, 1779, Woodhull recorded that there was a specific "[lady] of my acquaintance" so situated as to "out wit them all." Her sudden appearance in his letters following the recruitment of Townsend, as well as the fact that Townsend's ledger shows he and Woodhull met that same day, hints at the fact that she may have been introduced to the ring by Townsend himself. That she was already in Woodhull's acquaintance indicates that her name, at least, was already known to him prior to that day, perhaps indicating that she or her family were originally from Long Island. But her apparent presence in Manhattan of late meant that she was somehow uniquely positioned to collect important secrets in a cunning and charming manner that would leave those she had duped completely unaware that they had just been "outwitted" by a secret agent.

But just who was this mysterious woman so perfectly poised to steal such vital secrets? Woodhull was careful not to record her name, offering only a number—355—in the code that was to define the Culper Ring.

CHAPTER 7

Creating a Code

E ven as Robert Townsend was settling into his new role, something happened that highlighted the precarious nature of the world in which he now lived. On July 2, 1779, British raiders had attacked Major Tallmadge's camp at dawn, killing ten men and capturing eight, plus a dozen horses. Those losses were devastating, but in the aftermath Tallmadge made a discovery that proved unsettling and was potentially threatening to the Patriots' intelligence operations. One of the horses the British had stolen was his own, which still bore its saddlebags and some of Tallmadge's personal papers—including some money earmarked for Woodhull and a letter from Washington that specifically named George Higday, a resident of Manhattan "who I am told hath given signal proofs of his attachment to us, and at the same time stands well with the enemy."

Eleven days later, Higday was arrested at his home and confessed to having met with General Washington to discuss the possibility of spying, but claimed that he never carried out any such activity because the payment had been in fake bills. There is no record of any punishment carried out against Higday; he was probably deemed harmless and sufficiently terrified not to be tempted into any covert actions in the future, so the matter was dropped. But Washington had now seen the dangers of using real names in correspondence and, again, felt the weight of the responsibility he had to guard the lives of those risking themselves for their shared cause.

Beyond Higday's fate, there was another, even more immediate concern to the Culpers. On June 13, Washington had written to Tallmadge in regular ink and mentioned having a particular, special "liquid." What was further, he referred to "C——r," a common form of address for the day when a name was well known between two correspondents. The letter was intercepted and landed in the hands of the British *prior* to the July second raid, alerting them to the definite presence of an American spy in New York—one with whom Tallmadge was in close contact. The British had no way of knowing if C——r was a code name or a proper one, but they didn't care. They were after bigger fish than just a spy; they wanted the spymaster himself, and the seized letter pointed straight to his camp.

Though Tallmadge had been fortunate enough to escape capture, he knew that damage had been done. If the ring were to survive, the spies would have to disguise information to protect it from prying eyes while keeping it understandable to those who depended upon the contents of the letters.

Alarmed by the two close calls, Tallmadge turned to

the development of a code with a new sense of urgency. The ring had already begun to use a few numerical substitutions in their letters: for example, 10 stood for New York and 20 for Setauket, so that the recipient would know the source of the information contained in the reports. Two additional numbers, 30 and 40, were used to designate Jonas Hawkins and Austin Roe as post riders delivering the messages to their next destination. Tallmadge realized how essential it was that a more complete lexicon be developed and that every member or associate of the ring have a number rather than just a code name. In a style of cryptography developed originally by the French, Tallmadge selected a book and got to work. Making a list from 1 to 763, he pored over his copy of *Entick's Spelling Dictionary,* the 1777 London edition, and assigned each pertinent word, location, or name a numeric code. He became 721, Woodhull as Culper Senior 722, Townsend as Culper Junior 723, Roe 724, and Brewster 725. General Washington was 711 and his British counterpart, General Clinton, was 712. Numbers were often represented by letters, so that the year "1779," for example, might read as "ennq." If a word needed to be made plural, or put in the past or future tense, a "flourish" would be written on top of it to designate the change.

The new system was not foolproof and required some adjustments on the part of the users, but Woodhull and Tallmadge were able to use it to correspond comfortably within a few weeks, though with a lingering sense of concern for what damage had been done by the intercepted message in June. In his same letter

that mentioned the "[lady] of my acquaintance,"
Woodhull opened:

729 29 15th 1779

Sir. *Dqpeu Beyocpu agreeable to 28 met 723
not far from 727 & received a 356, but on his
return was under the necessity to destroy the
same, or be detected.... Thers been no augmentation by 592 of 680 or 347 forces, and
everything very quiet. Every 356 is opened at
the entrance of 727 and every 371 is searched,
that for the future every 356 must be 691 with
the 286 received. They have some 345 of the
route our 356 takes. I judge it was mentioned
in the 356 taken or they would not be so 660.*

Translated, and with a few creative grammatical
adjustments required by the reader, the letter conveyed the following message:

Setauket August 15th 1779

Sir. *Jonas Hawkins agreeable to appointment. Met Culper Junior not far from New
York & received a letter, but on his return was
under the necessity to destroy the same, or be
detected.... [There's] been no augmentation
by ship of war or land forces, and everything
very quiet. Every letter is opened at the
entrance of New York and every man is*

searched, that for the future every letter must
be write [written] with the ink received. They
have some know [knowledge] of the route our
letter takes. I judge it was mentioned in the let-
ter taken or they would not be so vigilant.

AGENT 355

Tallmadge's code contained a quirk that both reflects its time and offers up clues to a mystery. There are different codes to designate "man" (371) and "gentleman" (237), and "woman" (701) and "lady" (355); thus, there was a kind of commentary upon the social situation of a subject embedded within the code itself. Any mature adult might be referred to with the generic term "man" or "woman," according to the subject's sex; however, a "gentleman" in the American colonies was nearly always considered a man who owned land or a considerable amount of property, and was respected as a person of character in his local community. A woman might be referred to as a "lady" if she was of a well-to-do family, or was an accomplished young woman (that is, either literate and educated, or proficient in the arts of domestic leisure such as music, painting, and needlework). In other words, a man or a woman would generally only be referred to as a gentleman or a lady if he or she were of certain means and social standing. Social standing directly affected the quality of information a person could acquire: a washerwoman or a coachman might have been in a position to overhear some kinds of private conversations, whereas an established gentleman or lady might have been introduced to different types of gossip in a dining room, so Tallmadge's differentiation was strategic.

In the case of 355 (the "lady" of the Culpers' acquaintance), her code indicates that she was of some degree of social prominence. Was she Anna Smith Strong, the wife of Judge Selah Strong, a fierce Patriot who was first detained on a British prison ship in New York Harbor, then fled to Connecticut after his release? Local legend has it that Mrs. Strong, who remained behind to manage the house and family when her husband went into exile, used to hang laundry in specific patterns on her line. The Strong estate, situated on a high bluff, would be visible to anyone passing by boat across the Devil's Belt portion of Long Island Sound. The hanging clothes would appear as just that—wet clothes drying in the sun—to the untrained eye, but to Caleb Brewster, the arrangement of garments and their colors signified different counts of ships and troops, or in which cove it was safe for him to dock his boat, depending on which version of the story one hears. He would then be able to compile this information and pass it on with the Culper letters from New York when he rowed back across the water to meet Tallmadge or his courier in Connecticut.

While Anna Smith Strong might have played a satellite role in the ring—she was certainly an acquaintance of many of its members—assisting Woodhull, Roe, or Brewster at some point, there is no actual evidence that either she or her laundry ever served their country by gathering or passing along intelligence. It seems quite unlikely that the fortyish housewife, mother, and spouse of a well-known Patriot rabble-rouser would have ventured from Long Island to Manhattan to attend parties where she would have rubbed elbows with the Loyalist elite and gained the trust of high-ranking British officers.

A much more likely contender would be a young woman living a fashionable life in New York. Though of pro-American sentiments herself, she almost certainly would have been attached to a prominent Loyalist family, either as a freethinking daughter or a cousin or a niece who was staying in the city with her Tory relations. It is therefore possible that 355 was part of the glittering, giggling cluster of coquettes who flocked about Major André as he moved around the city, enjoying the finest food, wine, and company New York had to offer. Some of New York's brighter blooms were demure and others played coy, but, just as had been the case in Philadelphia, a few found themselves admitted into André's private chambers and his confidence, too.

BEYOND LETTERS

Despite the white ink and the coded communications, Washington knew that the British were growing more suspicious of the mail and that the tiniest details could attract scrutiny. Writing from his headquarters at West Point, New York, Washington sent Tallmadge a letter advising the major on this matter and also suggesting that Townsend not sacrifice his current employment in order to operate full-time as a spy. His cover story, as it stood, protected him far better and allowed him more freedom to gather information than he would have if he focused solely on intelligence gathering. The letter reveals much of General Washington's thought process concerning espionage, especially in regard to protecting his valued source.

> Head-Quarters, West Point,
>
> 24 September, 1779.
>
> Sir,
>
> *It is not my opinion that Culper Junior should be advised to give up his present employment. I would imagine that with a little industry he will be able to carry on his intelligence with greater security to himself and greater advantages to us, under cover of his usual business, than if he were to dedicate himself wholly to the giving of information. It may afford him opportunities of collecting intelligence that he could not obtain so well in any other manner. It prevents also those suspicions which would become natural should he throw himself out of the line of his present employment. He may rest assured of every proper attention being paid to his services. One thing appears to me deserving of his particular consideration, as it will not only render his communications less exposed to detection, but relieve the fears of such persons as may be entrusted with its conveyance to the second link in the chain, and of course very much facilitate the object we have in view; I*

mean, that he should occasionally write his information on the blank leaves of a pamphlet, on the first, second, and other pages of a common pocket book, or on the blank leaves at each end of registers, almanacks, or any new publication or book of small value. He should be determined in the choice of these books principally by the goodness of the blank paper, as the ink is not easily legible unless it is on paper of a good quality. Having settled a plan of this kind with his friend, he may forward them without risk of search or the scrutiny of the enemy, as this is chiefly directed against paper made up in the form of letters.

I would add a further hint on this subject. Even letters may be made more subservient to this communication, than they have yet been. He may write a familiar letter on domestic affairs, or on some little matters of business, to his friend at Setauket or elsewhere, interlining with the stain his secret intelligence, or writing it on the opposite blank side of the letter. But that his friend may know how to distinguish these from letters addressed solely to himself, he may always leave such as contain secret information without date or place (dating it with the stain), or fold them up in a particular manner, which may be concerted between the parties. This last appears to be the best mark of the two, and may be the signal of their being designated for me. The first mentioned mode,

*however, or that of the books, appears to me the
one least liable to detection. I am, &c.*

Washington, it seems, was an advocate of the practice of hiding messages in plain view. If a letter appeared suspicious or was treated with the utmost
caution and concern, it was more likely to tip off British inspectors. By instead passing along the highly
sensitive information disguised as dull letters on
day-to-day family news or hidden in a book, the vehi-
cle by which the message was being sent would probably not warrant a second glance. Only the intended
recipient would know, alerted by an otherwise mean-
ingless clue such as a specific fold, that there was anything more to the item than what met the eye.

With Rivington's print shop operating just down the
street, and as someone who enjoyed an established relationship with the owner, Townsend had no shortage of
books available for sending messages the way Washington had put forward. But Townsend, using his invisible
ink, seems to have preferred an alternative means of his
own design: When the courier (usually Woodhull or
Roe, judging from his store's ledger) arrived to pick up
the goods he had purchased to bring back to Long Island, among them would be a packet of blank writing
paper. Concealed within those loose leaves was a seemingly blank sheet that contained the invisible letter to be
rendered readable once it reached its destination and the
stain was applied. Clear communication as to how many
sheets into the stack the significant paper would be
placed was essential to avoid wasting precious reagent

in an attempt to discern which sheet contained the message, but all in all it worked extremely well as an innocuous way to smuggle reports out of the city.

With these new security measures in place, and Culper Junior and 355 firmly established in their roles in New York, the ring could now begin to forward intelligence more swiftly, safely, and in greater detail than before, though the risk of detection and capture remained. The life of a spy always requires looking over one's shoulder, but now Washington's operatives could enjoy at least a little more freedom to speak about their observances and advisements without needing to censor their words in case a letter fell into the wrong hands.

The added security was just in time, too, with André's arrival in the city. There were plots afoot—plans of deceit, treason, and betrayal—and the only hope the Americans had to survive them was to be prepared. Washington knew that New York City was of the utmost strategic importance from a military perspective, but even he could not anticipate how crucial the intelligence collected there would be in saving the cause for liberty. And neither side, American nor British, could yet imagine just how deep the treachery reached within its own ranks.

CHAPTER 8

Mounting Tensions and Double-Dealings

Suspicions and tensions were beginning to rise even as the summer of 1779 reached its peak, and all the agents were feeling the stress. Washington sent "all the white Ink I now have (indeed all that there is any prospect of getting soon)" with a trusted colonel, along with the desperate instructions:

> You will send these to C——r, Junr., as soon as possible, and I beg that no mention may ever be made of your having received such liquids from me or any one else. In all cases and at all times this procedure and circumspection is necessary, but it is indispensably so now as I am informed that Govr. Tryon [British governor of New York] has a preparation of the same acid or something similar to it, which may lead to a detection if it is ever known that a matter of this sort has passed from me.

Just four days later, Townsend prepared another letter for General Washington, closing with several lines that pointed to the increased danger he was also observing. "The times now are extreamly difficult," he wrote. "Guard boats are kept out every night in the North and East Rivers to prevent any boats from passing, & I am informed that some persons have been searched on Long Island; therefore, whenever you think that my intelligence is of no service, beg you will notify me."

Indeed, letters were now being searched with regularity as they left the city. Jonas Hawkins, the ring's sometime courier, twice believed he was in danger of being found out and destroyed the missives he was carrying from Townsend, much to the older man's annoyance.

On September 11, 1779, Woodhull acted as courier in place of Hawkins and wrote to explain what had happened to the letters from Culper Junior that had never made it to Washington as a result of Hawkins's fear. "The bearer thought himself in danger. I believe it was merely imaginary," Woodhull penned. "From timidity and the situation of affairs at the time, he did to choose to come to N.Yk; I therefore met him at a place quite out of danger on Long-Island. I then made an appointment . . . at wch. time he came, I wrote it, and took it over the Ferry that he might run no hazard from the Inspector of Letters there."

Townsend had never felt confident in Hawkins, having resented that his identity necessarily should be known by a boy he considered too immature for such serious work. For all of Townsend's natural reserve, his reaction was almost certainly far from calm.

"He should have never been entrusted with such a task!" Townsend stormed to Woodhull when he learned of the destruction of his second letter.

"We needed another courier," Woodhull tried to explain.

"But why am I risking my life gathering information day after day if my letters are to be destroyed before they reach the general?"

Woodhull shook his head. "The boy simply panicked."

"But one who panics—or even looks nervous—before the inspectors is bound to bring extra scrutiny upon himself. And if he is searched and anything suspicious is found upon him, where will be the first place the British turn?" He paused, looking to Woodhull for an answer, but Woodhull just scraped at a bit of candle wax on the table. "They'll look to any of his known associates, and to the last place he did business which, inevitably, will bring them to my shop," Townsend finished, flatly.

"We are, all of us, on edge," Woodhull said quietly.

"And we are, all of us, endangered by that boy's want of good sense and composure." Townsend banged his fist upon the table with such force it caused the candles to jump.

"I cannot always be coming here to retrieve your information myself. That will raise suspicions, too," Woodhull insisted. "Besides, General Washington desires the information even more quickly than we have been supplying it. If you wait until I am able to make the trip, it will only delay the relay of news."

"Then we get another man," Townsend said, sighing and sinking into the straight-backed chair. "This time one who knows how to keep his wits about him."

"But you were the one who insisted that your identity not be disclosed to anyone else. So what are we to do?"

Townsend dropped his head into his hands. The two friends discussed several scenarios, weighing the risks and benefits of each. Finally, they thought of Amos Underhill, Woodhull's brother-in-law and the proprietor of the boardinghouse where Woodhull stayed on his frequent trips to Manhattan.

"He needs provisions as much as anyone else. Why could he not frequent my shop for goods and pick up the reports at the same time?" Townsend mused.

Woodhull considered this. "I'd still have to travel into the city to retrieve them, unless Amos could be convinced to come across the water sometimes."

"But it would lessen your visits to my shop, and give us fewer opportunities to be spotted together. And he need not know the exact nature of our business together unless you deem it absolutely necessary."

"It's a gloomy thing to toast on," Woodhull remarked. "But I agree that it's a far better thing than to have young Hawkins destroy any more of your letters or, worse, be driven to madness and confess all. Give me a bit of time to present the matter to Amos and make proper arrangements. Until then, I will continue to serve as courier."

One can hardly blame Hawkins for his trepidation; the threats were growing and the whole Culper Ring felt the squeeze. The pressure continued to mount as autumn approached. Besides fearing British searches, the couriers also faced dangers from increasingly active privateers. In his letter dated November 1, 1779, Tallmadge wrote to General Washington of the growing hazards faced by members of the ring, including the once-fearless Caleb Brewster: "The boat that crosses for dispatches from C—— has been chased quite across the Sound by those plunderers, perhaps for the sake of being the more secret in their Villany, while our crew has suspected them to be the Enemy. Indeed if some stop cannot be put to such nefarious practices C—— will not risque, nor 725 [Brewster] go over for dispatches."

By the end of November, Amos Underhill's name began to appear regularly in Townsend's ledger. Hawkins, meanwhile, seems also to have questioned his involvement and quietly removed himself from the ring. Underhill's appearance could not have been better timed, as Woodhull's nerves were again getting the best of him. Woodhull had been questioned by a party of British troops while en route to meet up with Townsend at a safe house on Long Island, but apparently he kept his wits about him, because he was released without having to succumb to a more thorough search; Townsend, however, did not show. Woodhull waited at the rendezvous point the next day as well, but there was no sign of Culper Junior. The excuse for his absence does not appear in any of Townsend's letters, but as he was quite condemning in his correspondence of others who failed to make appointments, it was undoubtedly a serious matter beyond simply a lack of courage. The slip brought Woodhull nearly to a breaking point, prompting him to tell Tallmadge afterward that he had endured "a full year's anxiety, which no one can scarcely have an idea of, but those that experience. Not long since, there was not even the breadth of your finger betwixt me and death."

Woodhull's complaint was not unwarranted. The residents of Long Island were bracing for an even greater number of troops to be quartered there during the coming winter than they had endured the winter before; they also continued to absorb Loyalist refugees from all over the eastern seaboard. "The inhabitants of this Island at present live a miserable life, which you may readily judge when having the refuse of three kingdoms and thirteen States amongst them. Plundering and rapine increaseth at no small rate," Woodhull wrote in the same letter to Tallmadge. "I am tired of this business, it gives me a deal of trouble, especially when disappointments happen. Could not consent to be any longer an assistant if I was not almost an Enthusiast for our success."

But there was a covert storm brewing in New York—one that Townsend was in the process of uncovering and confirming—that threatened the Americans not through bloodshed or siege, but through their pocketbooks. And if it was on account of uncovering this business that Townsend was unable to meet up with Woodhull, he might very well be excused by reason of the magnitude of the plot he thwarted.

STRIKING A MINT

The British were highly skilled counterfeiters, and one of their favorite ways to attack the Americans was by depreciating colonial currency. At the most basic level, a worthless currency made it difficult for the Continental Army to purchase rations and rendered the soldiers' pay quite literally not worth the paper it was printed on. On a grander scale, having a wildly inflated currency made it nearly impossible for American diplomats overseas to secure credit with foreign banks—a severe problem in both the short and long terms. Without financial backing, the Americans could not bankroll the food, men, horses, war ships, and weapons needed to win the Revolution. If, against all odds, they were successful in their split from the British Crown, the new nation would need credit to rebuild its infrastructure—a concern the British did not have to contend with, because the war was an ocean away from London.

Recognizing the vulnerability of the American currency, the British ran counterfeiting operations aboard British ships and onshore where possible. Distribution of counterfeit bills was an open secret in the early years of the war, with advertisements even running in newspapers for travelers headed to other colonies to carry with them fake bills of their current location to their new destination. Aware of the danger, Woodhull himself even insisted on being paid in the king's currency—a request Washington honored without question.

The Continental Congress had made some efforts to combat the counterfeiting but saw limited success.

Eventually, they developed a special paper of a very precise quality and thickness that would be used to produce the bulk of the money minted in Philadelphia and, it was hoped, would be extremely difficult to replicate. This would allow the government much greater control as to the amount in circulation, which would, in turn, control inflation.

What Townsend learned, however, and wrote about with urgency to Washington on November 27, 1779, was that "several reams of the paper made for the last emissions struck by Congress have been procured from Philadelphia." The one safeguard upon which the Americans were counting to protect their currency had been breached. Somehow, whether through negligence or a double agent, the paper and possibly even the printer plates had made their way to New York, where the British could use them to churn out perfect counterfeits. Distribution in New York would drive down prices and sink the economy of the colonies right in the heart of their main trading hub. General Clinton, Major André, and their colleagues based in New York would meanwhile be feasting and dining on the unmatched power of sterling currency as the city—and the entire fledgling nation—crumbled around them.

Though the attempts to destroy the war effort through counterfeit bills were neither new nor secret, the magnitude of this particular plot and the fact that the worthless bills would be undetectable before it was too late made this intelligence of no small significance. With word from the Culpers delivered swiftly, Washington was able to alert Congress to the scheme. The resulting action—a cancellation of all colonial bills a few months later in March 1780—was drastic and potentially devastating in itself, but far less destructive to the American economy and morale than a sneak attack on its currency would have been.

Just how had Townsend uncovered such a plan? He may have happened upon some gossip by lucky coincidence, but the certainty with which Townsend outlined the plan for Tallmadge and Washington indicates that he had a much more intimate knowledge of the scheme than just hearsay. His source? The newest member of the ring.

THE MANY LIVES OF JAMES RIVINGTON: THE LAST PIECE

James Rivington, that same enterprising printer, newspaper editor, and coffeehouse owner with whom both Townsend and André had a friendship, was something of an American success story—though his path was far from typical. Whatever misfortunes he had suffered in England, his businesses were thriving in the New World and he was a master of spotting new opportunities. By the middle of the 1770s, his New York–based newspaper was being read at least as far south as Baltimore. When the sparks of revolution became the full-fledged flames of war in 1775, however, Rivington's shop was looted and burned by the Sons of Liberty, with some of his presses and typefaces being melted down for ammunition. He moved his family back to England for their own safety, then returned to New York in 1777, where he opened his businesses near Townsend's shop.

While Rivington was away, his surviving presses were busy serving the king without him. On June 26, 1776, a counterfeiter named Israel Young testified to having heard from a trusted source that a ship in New York waters, the *Duchess of Gordon,* had been the site of a counterfeiting workshop. What was more, Young recounted, the work was overseen by none other than New York's colonial governor, William Tryon. Young swore that he heard from his source that he "had also seen Governour Tryon often, and that the Governour would talk very free with them; that they had on board a number of Rivington's types and one of his printers." The source "received a letter which he said was from the Governour, and also some water-work money, which he said they counterfeited on board the *Duchess,* and he himself had seen them printing it off; that they had a chest of it."

Whether it was with Rivington's knowledge at the time or not, his name was thus linked with the counterfeiting trade and he undoubtedly drank free in British circles afterward for having such a reputation. Any rumors of counterfeiting schemes circulating among the British officer corps of New York would have certainly been considered of interest to Rivington, and he may have even been consulted as to the best way to carry out the endeavor. With Townsend in his employ and frequenting the coffeehouse, word of the plan could have easily slipped out either accidentally or as a matter of interest to the curious part-time reporter.

Or it might have been very deliberately shared.

As it turns out, there was much more to James Rivington, "Printer to the King's Most Excellent Majesty," than met the eye. At some point following his return to America from England at the end of 1777, it seems that his loyalties shifted. It remains unclear whether he was driven by a change of heart toward the American cause, a desire for monetary gain, or simply frustration at the Crown's objections and prohibitions to his printing criticisms of the leadership of General Howe in the autumn of 1778. But what is certain is that Rivington secretly threw in his lot with the Americans and began to work alongside Robert Townsend gathering information and conveying it outside the city to General Washington's waiting hands.

Rivington's name was the last to appear among the Culper code monikers, 726, indicating that Townsend had recruited him soon after his own engagement, probably by the late summer of 1779, when the code was developed. The code first lists the spies' names, concluding with Rivington as 726, then seamlessly moves on from personal names to place-names, with New York designated as 727. How so cautious and reserved a man as Townsend was able to establish a confidence with an avowedly Tory propagandist is hard to imagine. Once the connection was made, however, Rivington's mischievous nature must have delighted in the irony of his recruitment. This was the same man, after all, who found great amusement in seeing himself hung in effigy and who happily reprinted damning letters about his character from Patriot circulars in his own newspaper.

His unconventional sense of humor aside, Rivington proved a valuable asset to Townsend's work. Taking advantage of his profession, he provided books for the spies' use. Sometimes the books' bindings hid slips of paper holding intelligence Rivington himself had gleaned from his Loyalist guests and friends.

Several years later, William Hooper, a North Carolina lawyer who had signed the Declaration of Independence, wrote to his friend and future Supreme Court justice James Iredell:

> *It has come out as there is now no longer any reason to conceal it that Rivington has been very useful to Gen Washington by furnishing him with intelligence. The unusual confidence which the British placed in him owing in a great measure to his liberal abuse of the Americans gave him ample opportunities to obtain information which he has bountifully communicated to our friends.*

The British were being played, and from the least likely of corners. But they remained oblivious to the double-dealings in their midst. The parties went on. The coffeehouse debates continued as the officers went about surrounded by their circles of admirers. Major André's silly love poems were composed and published in Rivington's *Royal Gazette*. The wine and the words flowed freely as they bantered about their plans. The army was in garrison—comfortable, amused, and completely oblivious to the fact that any shopkeeper, newspaperman, or charming lady in their midst was listening, remembering, and plotting.

CHAPTER 9

Washington Demands More

N ow Washington had tasted victory; his agents had outsmarted the enemy in their own territory. It could be done. By revealing the counterfeiting plot, the Culper Ring had proved that New York was not some insurmountable fortress; they had penetrated its vault of secrets successfully and unmasked an entire plot before it could be played out to its catastrophic end. Best of all, the enemy had no way of knowing at what stage the plan may have been leaked or tracing back any breaches of secrecy. Washington's informants, therefore, were relatively safe from detection and could continue their activities without too much concern for their welfare.

Even so, there was much more afoot—of that Washington was certain. Now that one plan had been foiled another would soon be hatched, probably with more speed this time to minimize the risk of leaks. Some delicacy must be sacrificed for the sake of urgency, but could he make his most trusted, most valued, and most secretive ring understand that? He pored over the maps as he would before a battle; perhaps there was a way to convey messages across the Hudson River or via Staten Island? He wrote as much to Tallmadge, urging him to talk to Culper Senior about such an option, hoping to impress upon the ring the importance of timely reports.

The Culpers, meanwhile, were enjoying something of a reprieve from the oppressive worries that had plagued them of late. Colonel Simcoe had left his reluctant hosts, the Townsends, and led the Queen's Rangers back to the mainland in an effort to capture George Washington. They had failed, and Simcoe was now being held prisoner by the Americans. Woodhull, no doubt voicing the sentiments of numerous people, concluded his letter to Tallmadge on December 12, 1779: "Were I now in the State of New Jersey without fear of Law or Gospel, [I] would certainly kill Col. Simcoe, for his usage to me." In that same message, he included a blank sheet containing a stain letter from Townsend with whom he wrote he planned to celebrate Christmas.

Holiday leisure was a luxury the commander in chief could ill afford as the fate of the entire Revolution rested heavily upon his shoulders. Even as Woodhull wrote that his "fears are much abated," Washington felt a growing sense of urgency to see the cracks in New York's armor exploited even more aggressively. Matters in the southern colonies showed signs of deteriorating come spring, which meant that his attention and resources would be even more divided and strained. If the British were plotting any offensive maneuvers from the city, he wanted to be prepared.

Washington must have communicated his urgency to the ring, because Amos Underhill visited Townsend's shop with increased frequency starting in mid-January 1780, appearing in his ledger four times in just over three weeks. But the smuggled messages were not meeting the pressing demands Washington was facing. Events were accelerating rapidly, and the laborious means of conveying the letters out of occupied New York and Long Island, into Connecticut, and overland to Washington's camp were too slow. Instead of providing new information, the Culper Ring's intelligence was now providing verification of facts the general had already learned. "His accounts are intelligent, clear, and satisfactory, consequently would be valuable, but owing to the circuitous route through which they are transmitted I can derive no immediate or important advantage from them," Washington wrote Tallmadge on February 5. "And (as I rely upon his intelligence) the only satisfaction I derive from it, is, that other accts. are either confirmed or corrected by his, after they have been some time received."

He was not unsympathetic to the tremendous challenges his ring faced—most specifically, the risks Culper Junior, who lived and worked in the heart of the British operations, endured every day. "I am sensible of the delicacy of his situation, and the necessity of caution," Washington added to his letter, as if realizing the harsh tone of his criticism in the preceding lines directed to his favorite spy. He went on to suggest that he may be able to provide Culper Junior with more direct possibilities for moving the letters out of New York, though he acknowledged the risks involved in expanding the ring beyond its current members: "I have hitherto forborn and am yet unwilling to mention, persons to him as the vehicles of conveyance lest they should not prove so trustworthy and prudent as we could wish."

A few weeks later, Woodhull found himself writing back to Washington, informing the general of detailed ship movements, as well as warning him of even more potential risk from greatly increased scrutiny and enemy presence in Setauket: "Two regts. is to be stationed in this Town. If it should take place it will I fear entirely ruin our correspondence. To prevent which I shall give you early intelligence of their motions from time to time, that you may be prepared to give them a fatal blow at the beginning, or we shall be totally ruined."

The reprieve Woodhull's emotions had enjoyed in December had proved all too brief. It was March now, which meant increased activity could be anticipated with the spring thaw. But the winter of 1779–80, known as "the Hard Winter," proved to be one of the coldest recorded seasons of the eighteenth century in North America, and refused to let up. The weather took a turn for the worse, with tumultuous spring storms thwarting several efforts to convey letters to Washington explaining that the Culpers had taken seriously his concerns regarding the speed of their reports. Under increased pressure to perform, Woodhull once again let his nerves get the best of him as he attempted to count and recount the blank sheets of paper that had come to him as part of his last batch of goods from Townsend. Somehow, the number never seemed to come up right and the same sheet was never landed upon twice. Worried about sending a worthless paper rather than the one that contained the message written in the stain, Woodhull finally threw up his hands and dashed off a note: "*Sir.* Inclosed you have a blank—Something fearful not sending the right and have inclosed three."

THE MESSENGER DEBACLE

Meanwhile, Townsend looked for new couriers who could carry messages northward across the Hudson as the general had requested instead of across the Sound and through Connecticut. Rather than choose an outsider, he turned to a family member, a cousin named James Townsend, who was only sixteen or seventeen years old at the time. The young man had no idea as to the exact nature of the letters with which he was entrusted; he only knew that they contained sensitive information that was important to his grave, somber cousin—and that they would land him in prison if his mission was found out.

Armed with just enough ignorance to be safe, just enough knowledge to be cautious, and just enough bravery to be dangerous, James set off under the assumed identity of a Loyalist visiting relatives outside the city. His travels progressed smoothly until he stopped at the home of the Deausenberry family. He expected they would be sympathetic to giving him rest and shelter, as they were ardent Patriots in an otherwise Tory-dominated area, but James seems to have played his part as a Loyalist too convincingly. The Deausenberry daughters, young women about his own age, suspected that he might even be a Tory spy. In the hopes of causing him to spill his story, they pretended to be Loyalists, too, much to James's surprise. Confused by their switch, the boy feigned intoxication in the hopes of covering his tracks and convincing the family he was harmless, but it was too tangled of a web to escape by that point.

"Oh, I was within two miles of New York City the day before yesterday," he slurred, "carrying a number of stockings to my uncle and brother. I planned to join up with the British while I was there."

"Why ever didn't you?" one of the young ladies inquired.

"They told me I should come over here and recruit several more lads to join up with me so we could meet up with the British together when they head up the river in a week, as they are expected to do."

"And is that what you are endeavoring to do at present?"

"I've persuaded many a good fellow to enlist," James pushed on. "Very frequently over the course of the last summer I've been backward and forward to and from New York, having piloted several companies of British soldiers. I've carried in and brought out many valuable articles."

The young ladies affected appropriate reactions of admiration, which only emboldened James further. "Once I was taken upon by the damned rebels who left me confined and chained down, flat on my back in the Provost three weeks." The game was too fun, too delicious an opportunity for a red-blooded young man to resist embellishing his story, especially when he could do so with a clean conscience, believing it to be necessary to save both his life and his mission. He continued: "Finally, I made my escape by breaking out—"

With a roar, John Deausenberry, the elder brother of the two ladies, leapt from his hiding place and pounced upon James, declaring him a prisoner. A terrified James was immediately carted off to the American army camp nearby, where he was searched thoroughly, and John Deausenberry gave a full and detailed deposition on the matter. To the great disappointment of both the Deausenberrys and the soldiers, nothing of interest was found on James, though they did commandeer the two sheets of paper he was carrying that contained a groan-worthy poem called "The Lady's Dress" on a page folded in a peculiar manner and signed with a nearly illegible "S.T." The soldiers sent the letters on to headquarters, and James was held in Patriot custody.

Poor James's mission was not a complete debacle, because the papers did reach Washington. The general recognized the unusual manner of folding (his own suggestion from the September 24, 1779, letter) and knew the initials "S.T." indicated that stain was to be applied. The handwriting, too, was a giveaway that the papers had come from none other than Culper Junior. As Washington dabbed the stain between the lines of the poem (which humorously describes the elegance of a healthy-looking lady's apparel until a husband realizes his wife is half the size she appears once her hoops and many layers have been removed) Townsend's message began to appear. Unfortunately, it was almost completely unreadable and, before he even reached the end, Washington resolved to waste no more of his precious stain in an attempt to develop something that was inscrutable.

Even more frustrating to the general was that his personal involvement was required to secure James's freedom. Washington was furious that so much unnecessary attention had been drawn to covert operations, wasting resources and time on what proved to be an unfruitful mission. More than a little of the general's precious focus had to be diverted from strategy and planning to handling the matter with delicacy before James was finally released to slink back to New York with his tail between his legs. Tallmadge was briefed on the situation and he, in turn, made sure that Woodhull understood the depth of Washington's displeasure. That message, it seems, was received directly and not at all softened in tone.

TUMULTUOUS SPRING

Admittedly, Townsend's papers had reached their destination, but the whole embarrassing incident did nothing to boost anyone's confidence in the New York spies' ability to speed up the transmission of their intelligence. It even threatened a fissure within the ring itself; Woodhull was left making apologies and excuses for what he considered to be Robert Townsend's profound lack of judgment in recruiting James, while Townsend insisted that as the prime information gatherer it had been incumbent upon him to at least attempt a different mode of communication. The disagreement was sharp, and in the end proved nearly fatal to the ring. Woodhull wrote to Tallmadge on May 4, 1780, "I have had an interview with C. Junr. and am sorry to find he declines serving any longer."

Washington had had enough. New York continued to taunt him and no intelligence he had received of late offered any hope that he might be able to wage an attack soon. The ring's failure was no real fault of their own, and Washington knew there had been no lack of effort to meet his increasingly urgent requests, but the results were discouraging all the same. When the general learned that Culper Junior—the link in the ring whose intelligence he had once valued above that of all other agents in the employ of the Continental Army— wanted to withdraw, he decided the entire endeavor would be pointless without him. In frustration, he determined to start from scratch and build a new network.

From his headquarters in Morristown, New Jersey, he wrote to Tallmadge on May 19: "As C. Junior has totally declined and C. Senior seems to wish to do it, I think the intercourse may be dropped. . . . I am endeavoring to open a communication with New York

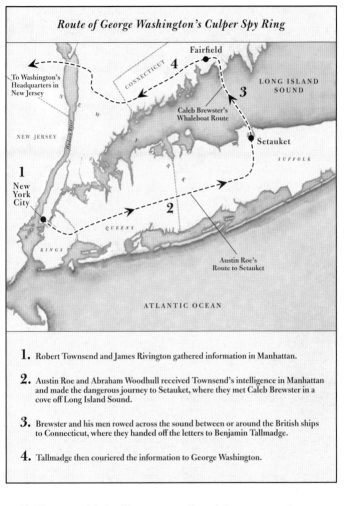

Route of George Washington's Culper Spy Ring

To Washington's Headquarters in New Jersey

CONNECTICUT

4 Fairfield

LONG ISLAND SOUND

3

Caleb Brewster's Whaleboat Route

Setauket

SUFFOLK

NEW JERSEY

Hudson River

1 New York City

2

QUEENS

KINGS

Austin Roe's Route to Setauket

ATLANTIC OCEAN

1. Robert Townsend and James Rivington gathered information in Manhattan.

2. Austin Roe and Abraham Woodhull received Townsend's intelligence in Manhattan and made the dangerous journey to Setauket, where they met Caleb Brewster in a cove off Long Island Sound.

3. Brewster and his men rowed across the sound between or around the British ships to Connecticut, where they handed off the letters to Benjamin Tallmadge.

4. Tallmadge then couriered the information to George Washington.

The secret six's intelligence route allowed them to transmit top-secret information from Manhattan through enemy territory to George Washington in about two weeks.

Benjamin Tallmadge, who fought side by side with George Washington, was tasked with forming the Culper Ring. His leadership and knowledge of Long Island made him indispensable.

Robert Townsend did not have the bravado of his older brother or his father, but his quieter heroic qualities made him the perfect spy leader—Culper Junior. True to his unassuming character, he seems never to have commissioned a painting of himself. This one rough sketch depicting him at age sixty is known.

James Rivington was the respected publisher of the *Rivington Gazette,* a loyalist newspaper. What the British didn't know was that he was also a spy for George Washington. With the help of Robert Townsend, he interviewed British officers about their military exploits and took their inside intelligence directly to Washington. Rivington's biggest contribution was acquiring the redcoats' battle plan for Yorktown. The colonists would beat Lord Cornwallis in that battle and win the war in the process.

Austin Roe's tavern still stands today, though it was moved from its original location. From here, Roe made the fifty-five-mile journey to Manhattan, passing through occupied Manhattan and Long Island to reach Robert Townsend.

The first man to sign on to the spying mission was Abraham Woodhull, known as Culper Senior. His detailed logbook enabled historians to put together many of his movements during the ring's years of operation. (Woodhull never wanted to be paid for spying but did want to be reimbursed for his expenses, one of the reasons his log entries were so detailed and accurate.) After the war, he became a respected judge but never spoke about his days in the Culper Ring. No portrait of Abraham Woodhull exists today, but his grave reflects his eminent position as a judge and his anonymity as a spy.

I / J		K / L		M / N		O / P	
i	280	July	336	mot	382	on	433
if	281	jug	337	mine	383	or	434
in	282	jury	338	many	384	out	435
is	283	jealous	339	mercy	385	offer	436
it	284	justify	340	moment	386	office	437
ice	285	january	341	murder	387	owed	438
ink	286			manner	388	order	439
into	287	**K**		method	389	over	440
instance	288	key	342	mischief	390	obstruct	441
island	289	king	343	mistake	391	obtain	442
impress	290	kill	344	molest	392	observe	443
improve	291	know	345	majesty	393	occur	444
encamp	292			meditate	394	offence	445
incur	293	**L**		memory	395	omit	446
infest	294	lars	346	messenger	396	oppose	447
inforce	295	land	347	misery	397	obligate	448
instance	296	love	348	moveable	398	obstinate	449
inward	297	low	349	multitude	399	obviate	450
extract	298	lot	350	miscarry	400	occupy	451
intrigue	299		351	mortotum	401	operate	452
interest	300	light	352	miserable	402	origin	453
instant	301	earl	353	monenary	403	ornament	454
invest	302	learn	354	majority	404	overcome	455
invite	303	lady	355	minority	405	overlook	456
ignorant	304	letter	356	memorial	406	overtake	457
impudent	305	levy	357	mistrian	407	overrun	458
industry	306	common	358	manufacture	408	overthrow	459
infamous	307	liar	359	moderate	409	obedience	460
influence	308	lucky	360	ministerial	410	objection	461
infantry	309	language	361			october	462
infantry	310	lentil	362	**N**		obscure	463
injury	311	liquid	363	name	411	occasion	464
innocent	312	longitude	364	new	412	opinion	465
instrument	313	latitude	365	no	413	oppression	466
intimate	314	laudable	366	note	414	opportunity	467
illegal	315	legible	367	night	415	obligation	468
imagin	316	liberty	368	never	416		
important	317	lottery	369	needful	417	**P**	
environ	318	literature	370	number	418	pay	469
introduce	319			neither	419	peace	470
november	320	**M**		nothing	420	plan	471
inhuman	321	man	371	neglect	421	put	472
inquiry	322	map	372	nation	422	port	473
interview	323	may	373	navy	423	proof	474
intersect	324	march	374	natural	424	please	475
intercede	325	marl	375	negative	425	part	476
interfere	326	make	376	negligence	426	paper	477
intermit	327	met	377	novemt	427	pardon	478
introduce	328	me	378	necessary	428	party	479
immediate	329	my	379	nobility	429	perfect	480
impatient	330	much	380				
management	331	move	381	**O**			
isolation	332			oath	430		
irregular	333			of	431		
	334			off	432		
indians	335						

30742

As the war heated up, the cover for the secret six grew deeper. First they used invisible ink, then code numbers, and finally they used both, writing in invisible ink between the lines in books using the code number system. This page from one of the few codebooks invented by and issued to the secret six demonstrates how the spies replaced places and people with numbers.

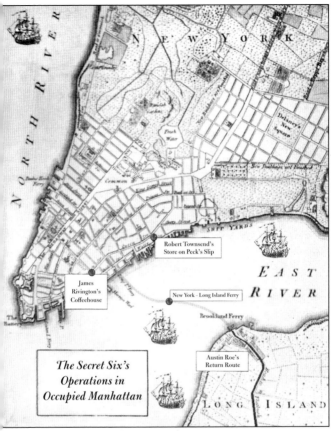

The Secret Six's
Operations in
Occupied Manhattan

Robert Townsend's
Store on Peck's Slip

James
Rivington's
Coffeehouse

New York - Long Island Ferry

Brookland Ferry

Austin Roe's
Return Route

Robert Townsend's business, Templeton & Stewart, was just a few
blocks from Rivington's *Gazette* office, with the Long Island ferry
dock located conveniently between the two.

Major John André, a charismatic ladies' man, ran a British spy ring and ultimately lost his life because of it. After his capture, he tried to negotiate a prisoner swap for himself, but General Washington had only one deal in mind: a swap of André for Benedict Arnold. After that was rejected, André was hanged on October 2, 1780.

Collection of the New-York Historical Society

Benedict Arnold is known for being a traitor but before that was best characterized as a respected battlefield general. His expectation that the colonists would lose the war and his bitterness over his belief that Congress owed him money together prompted him to secretly join the British. Had he succeeded in handing over West Point to the redcoats, Washington would have lost the Hudson River and most certainly the war. The Culpers tipped off Washington to Arnold's traitorous ways and thwarted the plot.

MAJ GEN BENEDICT ARNOLD

B. Arnold M Gen

Collection of the New-York Historical Society

In addition to West Point, Arnold hoped to deliver George Washington into British hands as well. He sent important intelligence back to Manhattan with Major John André, who was code named John Anderson. The note shown here ultimately cost André his life when Patriots intercepted him and found it in his boot. André himself later drew the self-portrait below the note on the day before his execution.

In 1783, George Washington and his army returned to New York City in victory. He would return as president seven years later and would govern the country from Manhattan. Major Tallmadge asked the general to delay his entry so that he could secure members of the ring, because many thought they were loyal to the king and they could be harmed unless protected.

Robert Townsend's grave, located on the edge of the Townsend family burial site up against a fence, is startlingly nondescript. Townsend wouldn't have wanted it any other way: an unassuming man, he lived and died without revealing his key role as one of George Washington's most successful and essential spies.

across Staten Island, but who are the agents in the City, I do not know." A few other spies were acting independently in the city, among them a tailor named Hercules Mulligan, who picked up gossip while measuring English soldiers for uniforms and suits, as well as Daniel Diehel, a man of Woodhull's acquaintance. No one compared to the finely tuned and proven Culper Ring, but they were almost all Long Islanders, and could operate most safely in their own environs. Their familiarity with the people and waterways had kept them from discovery thus far. If Washington thought a diversion of route to Staten Island was necessary to speed the delivery of the messages, then he must find spies who could navigate that island instead. It was just that simple. As far as he was concerned, the Culper business was finished, even if it had concluded on a somewhat sour note.

This news wounded Woodhull deeply. He replied to Tallmadge on June 10 in a tone that reads almost like that of a jilted lover trying to maintain dignity after an affair:

> I am happy to find that 711 [Washington] is about to establish a more advantageous channel of intelligence than heretofore. I perceive that the former he intimates hath been of little service. Sorry we have been at so much cost and trouble for little or no purpose. He also mentions of my backwardness to serve. He certainly hath been misinformed. You are sensible I have been indefatigable, and have done it from a principal of

duty rather than from any mercenary end—and
as hinted heretofore, if at any time theres need
you may rely on my faithful endeavours. I per-
ceive there's no mention made of any money to
discharge the remaining debts, which hath in-
creased since I saw you, owing to your direction
to continue the correspondence regular until I
received your answer from 711.

It is no wonder that the Culper communications had proved so disappointing to General Washington in the spring of 1780. The difficulties of delivering the messages in a timely fashion given the geographical constraints and weather were real, but the other reality was that there was little reliable information to be sent. General Clinton had left the city for South Carolina, taking the key decision makers with him. Even if the spies had been at the top of their game, they still would have had little news for Washington.

Agent 355 found herself in an especially difficult position. Only camp women and wives traveled with officers on the move—no respectable single woman would ever follow the soldiers, and certainly not a lady of her social standing. In the absence of the officers, whatever intelligence she was gleaning from whispered conversations with André, or from plots carelessly (or cockily) mentioned in passing, completely dried up. Townsend, for his part, could continue to chat with soldiers in his shop or make his inquiries at the docks and around the city as he inspected cargo ships for their wares or interviewed people for his newspaper column. Rivington could continue passing on bits of gossip he collected as a newspaperman and coffeehouse owner. But 355 could only await the return of her sources and the revival of her set before she could impart any further information.

Clinton's absence was short-lived. Charleston fell much the same way Manhattan had, and Clinton felt no need to stay to put down the backwoods colonists still causing trouble in the Appalachians. He would leave that to his officers and return to the metropolitan delights of New York: mistresses, theaters, balls, and the satisfaction of being the toast of one of the largest cities on the continent.

There was another reason why General Clinton hastened back to the glittering pleasures of New York in June 1780. Rumor had reached his ears that a fleet of French ships carrying troops was bound for North America. As complacent as he was, this new development troubled him. With the assistance of the French, the Americans might be able to take back New York— or even win the war without the city.

CHAPTER 10

The French Connection

General Washington could not hold a grudge for long. After cooling off for several weeks and realizing that no real harm had been done by the misadventures of James Townsend, he began to reconsider his decision. Slow but credible intelligence was better than fast but muddled—or no intelligence at all. Washington had grown accustomed to his reliable and detailed reports from the Culper Ring; those messages provided him with a sense that *something* was happening to advance the Patriot cause in New York, even if he was powerless to lead the charge to recapture the city.

Meanwhile, the same rumor that Clinton had heard grew to a buzz. A fleet of French ships was crossing the Atlantic at that very moment, coming to give the Americans a much-needed boost of men, might, and morale. If the British intercepted them it would be devastating.

Washington did not know where the French would land. He did not know whether the British knew, and, if they did know, how General Clinton was planning to ambush the fleet. Even great men make mistakes, and Washington knew he had committed a grave one in ending the spy ring. Never before, he realized, had he needed eyes and ears in New York so urgently. It had taken a long time to win over France, and the Americans could not afford to squander their new ally's good favor.

LOUIS XVI'S SECRET WAR

After centuries of warfare and uneasy truces both on home soil and in colonies abroad, the French wanted nothing more than to see the British defeated in the New World. Not only would it be beneficial for French claims in North America, but the humiliation heaped on King George for his loss to a bunch of upstart colonials was too delicious an opportunity for Louis XVI to ignore. The defeat of Britain in the American colonies would mean good things for France, and Louis was astute enough to realize that such a defeat would not be possible without outside assistance.

What was there to lose by offering help to the rebels? The British hated the French anyway, and the feeling was mutual, so French involvement would not poison any wells that were not already amply tainted. And what could be a more convenient means of deflating the British than supporting a war fought on someone else's soil, displacing someone else's population and destroying someone else's infrastructure?

As early as 1776, the fictitious Roderigue Hortalez &

Company trading house had smuggled French money and provisions into the colonies. The company bolstered the American cause prior to the formal declaration of independence from Britain, and continued to supply the colonists' needs until the French and Americans finalized a treaty. After Benjamin Franklin secured the Franco-American alliance in February 1778, the company had no need to operate undercover.

That is not to say French involvement had been invisible before the treaty was signed. A number of French military officers joined the American cause; most notable was the Marquis de Lafayette, who had been serving with General Washington since 1777. Admiral Jean-Baptiste-Charles-Henri-Hector d'Estaing navigated a fleet of ships up from the West Indies to Rhode Island in 1778, where they engaged with the British in an attack on Newport. D'Estaing's expedition disappointed Washington: Not only was the battle something of a draw, but the fleet declined to attack the British navy stationed around New York. Unable to save Savannah, Georgia, from siege in September and October 1779, the fleet eventually sailed back to France, taking with it Washington's high hopes for a decisive naval engagement that would shift the momentum in his favor.

In the spring of 1780, word spread that another fleet had launched on April 6 from the port city of Brest. Code-named the Expédition Particulière (the British called it "Special Expedition"), the fleet was in charge of transporting more than six thousand troops under the command of Count Jean-Baptiste Donatien de Vimeur de Rochambeau. Both sides knew it had the potential to sway the outcome of the war.

That a large French fleet was sailing to the aid of the American cause was no secret in Europe; the extensive preparations for such a venture could scarcely be kept under wraps. But when and where the ships would land was a guessing game for both the Americans and the British. News of French plans had to travel by ship via almost exactly the same route as the fleet itself, making it nearly impossible to know ahead of time the destination of the reinforcements.

Washington had received intelligence that the fleet would be arriving soon and heading for Newport, Rhode Island. What he could not be sure of was whether the British knew the same thing or had only rumors and suspicions from which to operate. If the British were ignorant of the specifics, the Americans might have the element of surprise on their side. If the British had advance knowledge, they could move troops to engage the French as soon as they disembarked or even to prevent their landing in the first place.

By June, the British were in full-on preparation mode, making their best guesses and shoring up the areas they suspected to be the most vulnerable. In Woodhull's letter of June 10—the same in which he wrote with some offense toward Washington's revocation of the Culpers' duties—he also alerted Tallmadge to the flurry of activity on Long Island. "You speak with some assurance that the French is hourly expected to our assistance—hope they may not fail

us.... Ther's a grand movement on foot in N.York.
The troops are called from Lloyd's Neck and is said
from every other distant post, and an embargo laid on
all ships and small Sloops. It is suspected they are a
going to quite N.York, or are going to make some diversion up the river, or are afraid of the French. But I
cannot but think the former is likely to take place. For
I believe their whole design is to the Southward."

RACE TO NEW YORK

On July 11—and, unbeknownst to Washington, less
than twenty-four hours after the French ships dropped
anchor in Narragansett Bay, Rhode Island—Washington
sent an urgent letter to Tallmadge, asking him to reorganize the Culper Ring. "As we may every moment
expect the arrival of the French Fleet a revival of correspondence with the Culpers will be of very great importance," he scrawled, continuing:

> If the younger cannot be engaged again, you will
> endeavor to prevail upon the older to give you in-
> formation of the movements and position of the
> enemy upon Long Island—as whether they are
> all confined to the port at Brooklyn or whether
> they have any detached posts and where, and
> what is their strength at those posts—in short
> desire him to inform you of whatever comes un-
> der his notice and what seems worthy of commu-
> nication.

Tallmadge received the letter on July 14 and immediately replied to the general that he would set out the next morning to find Brewster, who was still regularly crossing Long Island Sound to Connecticut for trading and taunting purposes. He also made a delicate suggestion to Washington: "I would at the same time hint that by Cr's last letter, we are something in arrears to him, and in order to enable him to prosecute the business, it may be necessary to afford him a small supply of money."

Once located, Brewster eagerly set off to find Woodhull, who, unfortunately, was ill with a fever and could not travel (he might have been suffering from a nervous illness as well). Instead, Austin Roe leapt upon a horse and headed straight for New York to alert Townsend, an exhausting fifty-five-mile trip one way. Washington knew by now that the landing had occurred, and he realized that General Clinton would know, too. Townsend's mission was to spy out the British response to the fleet's arrival.

Roe waited in Manhattan four days while Townsend (and very likely Agent 355) made inquiries and gathered as much information as possible from their acquaintances among the British officers. Townsend then recorded the findings in invisible ink between the lines of an order form for goods from his store, and included a fake note apologizing that the merchandise was not available at the time but would be forwarded when it arrived. Roe carried the note back with him—a simple cover story as to why he was carrying papers but no merchandise, in case he should be searched—and gave the sensitive letter to Woodhull. Woodhull passed it on to Brewster that same night to row across the Sound, adding pressing directions: "The enclosed requires your immediate departure this day by all means let not an hour pass: for this day must not be lost. You have news of the greatest consequence perhaps that ever happened to your country."

Woodhull also submitted a summary of what he had heard as an adjunct to Townsend's findings, writing that the report

> *also assures of the arrival of Admiral Graves with six ships of the line and is joined by three more out of New York, also one of 50 and two of 40 guns and has sailed for Rhode Island and is supposed they will be there before this can possibly reach you. Also 8000 Troops are this day embarking at Whitestone for the before mentioned port. I am told for certain that the French have only seven sail of the line. I greatly fear their destination.*

Understanding the urgency, Woodhull decided to eliminate Tallmadge from the chain of communication, crossing his code name, John Bolton, off the address of one letter before handing the dispatch to Brewster, who rushed it straight to Washington's headquarters. Alexander Hamilton, Washington's closest aide, received the report on the afternoon of July 21.

Unflappable as ever, Washington received the information calmly and carefully considered the possibilities. He desperately wanted to capture New York City, and with Clinton leading most of the British troops stationed there northward to engage the French, this could be his best opportunity. But Washington also knew better than to act rashly. He called together several of his top officers, and they discussed the likelihood of a successful attack; the prevailing sentiment was that it would be unwise. Even with Clinton and a large number of his men gone, the city was still well fortified and the battle would end as a siege, giving Clinton time to return with his soldiers and engage the Americans. Regretfully, Washington was forced to agree with his counselors and admit that he must reject his ambitions to recapture the city, but the brilliant strategist realized he could still capitalize on Manhattan's vulnerability.

A DIRTY BUSINESS

Washington was always conscious that even as he had spies working behind the scenes, so must the British. Every move required a risk whose cost he must calculate. Each maneuver he planned that had the potential to outsmart the enemy could be countered by the British to the detriment of his own forces. Planting a little strategic information was the best way to protect his army against counterintelligence.

Satisfied with the decision not to attack New York, Washington dismissed his officers—and then hurriedly began drawing up plans and penning correspondence signaling a full-fledged attack upon Manhattan as soon as Clinton's forces were clear of the city and too near to Newport to be easily recalled. The parcel was dispatched with a courier who hastily left camp with very specific instructions on where and when to deliver the documents. Then Washington waited.

A few hours later, a man stumbled up to a British outpost with a bundle of papers. He told the soldiers he had found the bundle lying by the side of the road and assumed it had tumbled out of the poorly secured saddlebags of a rider traveling at breakneck speed. However it got there wasn't important, the British immediately concluded. A quick glance revealed battle plans for a pending attack on New York and letters outlining the strategy coming from the hand of Washington himself. The soldiers roused their senior officers, who quickly decided that Clinton and his troops must be recalled. Defeating the newly arrived French troops was important, but holding New York was doubly so.

Flares signaled the message to Clinton, and the British ships did an about-face to sail back to New York Harbor, where Clinton ordered his troops to brace the city for an attack that could come at any time. The whole city held its breath, every citizen straining to hear the first sound of cannon fire breaking the silence of the countryside as the Americans advanced.

They waited. And while they waited, the French disembarked and moved to an area of safety to await their marching orders with no interference from the British, no naval attacks upon their ships, and no ground offensives from Clinton's army. Washington's gamble had paid off beautifully.

George Washington, whom generations of school-children would later know as a man who "could not tell a lie," couldn't help but be pleased. Even if the victory was bittersweet, because his first choice would have been to recapture New York, he had been able to secure, through his design of a fake attack, the safe arrival of the French reinforcements, which would shore up his prospects for a more successful assault at New York or elsewhere in the future. By intentionally planting misinformation, he achieved on a grand scale what he had accomplished in a smaller way with John Honeyman at Trenton in December 1776.

As for the Culpers, the ring was securely back in Washington's good graces. The quality of their information and the prudence they exercised in delivering it had enabled him to both understand the plans of the British and take decisive action by choosing not to risk an attack on New York. The ring had more than proved its worth, but the war was not yet won.

CHAPTER 11

Benedict and Peggy

Even as the Americans were congratulating themselves on the success of their counterintelligence, a traitor was building his own network
within their midst. In the early summer of 1780, just as
the Culper Ring was entering its hiatus and Clinton and
André were settling back into New York after their foray
to South Carolina, Major General Benedict Arnold was
working to get his hands on a new command. Though
he had been living the high life in Philadelphia, some
recent unpleasantness had wounded his ego, and he
had found himself in an all-too-familiar position: humiliated, angry, and desperate to prove his worth. He
was about to show the world just how important he really was. If the Americans couldn't see his value, the
British would.

Arnold had been a man with something to prove
right from the start. Despite his current rank of major
general in the Continental Army, he was profoundly in-
secure and carried a chip on his shoulder from a lifetime

of feeling perpetually slighted by fate. Given the paternal name of "Benedict" after an older brother bearing the same name died in childhood, Arnold started out life living in the shadow of someone else, and no matter his later successes, he always seemed plagued by insecurities and a sense of somehow always falling short.

Unable to attend Yale due to his father's financial woes brought on by alcoholism and poor health, Arnold was forced to learn a trade instead. He apprenticed with two of his maternal uncles in their apothecary and mercantile shop but longed for something greater. In 1755, at the age of fourteen, he begged to be allowed to join the colonial militia that was in service of the king of England in the French and Indian War. His mother forbade him to do so, but two years later he enlisted anyway, only to leave the militia the following year, allegedly deserting.

However he came to be separated from his first term of military service, he proved to have a strong business sense and by his early twenties was running a successful pharmacy and bookshop in New Haven, Connecticut. Eventually he was able to purchase partial ownership in a small fleet of merchant ships and occasionally sailed on trading ventures to the Caribbean. With the increase of British taxation, starting with the Sugar Act in 1764 and the Stamp Act the next year, Arnold felt the pinch but followed the example of many American merchants who simply ignored the laws they viewed as unwarranted and unjust from a government that taxed its colonial citizens without granting them representation in Parliament.

In 1767, he married Margaret Mansfield, a hard-working and prudent woman who proved a valuable partner to him, thanks in large part to her family's solid standing in New Haven, where her father served as sheriff. Arnold began to fall on financial hard times and accumulated some substantial debts, but he continued in his trading business even as his outrage over the political climate in the colonies increased. On March 5, 1770, British soldiers fired into a crowd of protesters in Boston, killing five civilians and wounding six. The Boston Massacre infuriated Arnold. He had been in the West Indies at the time, so the news did not reach him until more than a month after the fact, but it stirred in him a profound sense of action and responsibility. "Good God," he wrote on June 9. "Are the Americans all asleep & tamely giving up their glorious liberties or, are they all turned philosophers, that they don't take immediate vengeance on such miscreants; I am afraid of the latter."

In March 1775, Arnold joined the Connecticut militia as a captain and just two months later received a colonel's commission in the Massachusetts Committee of Safety after he offered plans for attacking the British outpost at Fort Ticonderoga in northern New York. The mission was a success and Arnold garnered accolades for his performance, but he resigned his commission after a disagreement with another militia leader. He then set out to return home to serve in Connecticut. Bad news seemed to have a way of reaching Arnold whenever he was traveling, and he was on the road when he learned his wife had died.

Over the next few years, Arnold was involved in a number of key American victories and distinguished himself as an insightful strategist and able officer. But his talents were not nearly so celebrated as Arnold believed was his due. His advice was often heeded, though he was not sought out as a leader; he was passed over for command and promotion several times, which deeply wounded his ego. He became a polarizing figure, either loved or loathed by his comrades in arms. Those who argued in his favor pointed to his keen understanding of strategy and shrewd assessments of the enemy's vulnerabilities. Those who argued against him pointed to his quick temper, his growing pessimism toward the success of the American war effort, and his apparent motivation by personal glory and gain. Colonel John Brown, one of Arnold's rivals, prophetically wrote of him in 1777: "Money is this man's God, and to get enough of it he would sacrifice his country."

After distinguishing himself in the Battles of Saratoga in the fall of 1777, Arnold believed he had finally shamed his critics and detractors who were standing in the way of the meteoric rise he so desperately desired. His valor in combat was undeniable—even though he had acted in direct defiance of an order from his superior officer, with whom he had a personal dispute. He had been severely wounded in his left leg but refused to allow an amputation; instead, he had it set to heal, but the job was poorly done. As a result, Arnold walked with a limp for the rest of his life.

In June 1778, as the Americans were reestablishing

their presence in Philadelphia—and roughly two months before Woodhull began spying in New York as Culper Senior—Washington appointed Arnold the military commander of Philadelphia. Arnold quickly realized that this new position would allow him to engage in a variety of business deals to restore his finances, which were still plagued by his numerous debts back home in New Haven. He was not particularly popular among many citizens of Philadelphia, however, and complaints were soon raised that not all of his ventures were legitimate. One vocal critic was Allen McLane, a highly respected and distinguished soldier from Delaware, who had been among the first Americans to enter Philadelphia when the British left; McLane voiced his concerns to General Washington but was reprimanded for challenging such a high-ranking officer. When Arnold learned about the complaints, he was angry that so many citizens and fellow soldiers questioned his integrity, particularly because his position was one of public service to a war-torn city. Was he not an officer of the Continental Army who was fighting for the liberty and freedom of all Americans?

This upturn in his fortunes pleased Arnold, and he lived well in Philadelphia, even under the shadow of accusations that his gains were ill gotten. Like his British predecessors, he enjoyed rich furnishings and luxurious dinners and entertainments. He even mingled with Philadelphia's society belles, one of whom, Peggy Shippen, especially caught his attention.

PEGGY

As the youngest surviving child born into a politically prominent family, Margaret "Peggy" Shippen grew up a pampered, spoiled darling of her parents and blossomed into one of the stars of Philadelphia's social scene. Under her father's supervision, she received an excellent education, even dabbling in political theory, which was highly unusual for a young woman of her time but later made her a delight at dinner parties and a favorite conversant among the military officers quartered in the city.

The Shippens were devout Loyalists living in the midst of what was, in many ways, the heart of the American cause. Philadelphia had hosted the First Continental Congress in 1774, which convened in response to the Intolerable Acts imposed as punishment on the colonists by the British Parliament after the Boston Tea Party. In May 1775, the Second Continental Congress was called, and again the delegates met in Philadelphia. The city played host to several of the delegates' meetings over the next six years, including their most famous, in 1776, which resulted in the Declaration of Independence, all while the Shippens—and many other residents who considered themselves loyal to King George—looked on in disapproval.

When the British marched on Philadelphia in September 1777 and captured it easily, the Shippens and their friends welcomed them. The winter that followed, while miserable for the Americans encamped outside the city at Valley Forge, was rather delightful for the British soldiers stationed in town. Galas and dinners were hosted in honor of the officers, who were the centerpiece of the social scene. Major John André, the dashing British poet-spy who would later be published by Rivington in New York, was one of the most sought after, and he attracted a bevy of female followers wherever he went.

Seventeen-year-old Peggy was among André's admirers, and history hints that her attentions might have been returned. Members of the leisure class understood that flirtation was a lovely game when both parties engaged in it merely for sport; so when the British decided to abandon Philadelphia nine months later in order to shore up their defenses in New York, there were probably very few tears shed on Peggy Shippen's pillow. The dapper André had marched away, but nature, armies, and young hearts all abhor a vacuum, and the American troops who were now pouring into the city promised their own diversions and charms for the young lady.

AN UNLIKELY UNION

Peggy Shippen found her life little changed with the arrival of the Continental Army. Her family still had wealth and prestige, and the most significant alteration to the social scene was simply the color of the officers' jackets. Despite her family's political allegiances, Peggy soon found herself enamored with the widowed Patriot general Benedict Arnold, even though he was

nearly twenty years her senior. For his part, he was flat-
tered by the attentions of the young and vivacious
woman who remained one of the most prominent ladies in Philadelphia.

Just what the attraction was on Peggy's side is unclear. Arnold had position and prestige, but he also
had some fairly substantial debts, a military career that
might be in peril due to his wounded leg, a short temper, and deep-seated insecurities. Perhaps this was
precisely what made Arnold's Samson the perfect
catch for Peggy's Delilah. Peggy was a woman with a
mind of her own, and she may have realized just how
much power she could wield over such a husband. He
would, in essence, be her slave, bending himself to her
will out of fear that she might cuckold him if she didn't
get her way. If there was one thing Arnold craved, it
was admiration, and Peggy knew he thought that a
beautiful young wife on his arm would win him the
envy of his rivals.

Whatever the case, she captured his notice and his
heart, and the two were married the following April, in
1779. Arnold's life had never been better: His finances
were improving, both through his own investments
and through the fortune of his pretty new wife. He was
finally garnering the kind of respect and authority he
felt he deserved. Still, he was bitter because other
American officers seemed to be more popular and
loved by their men. Just one month after his marriage
to Peggy, an indignant Arnold wrote to General Washington regarding the charges against his business
practices in Philadelphia: "If your Excellency thinks

me criminal, for Heaven's sake let me be immediately tried, and, if found guilty, executed. I want no favor; I ask only for justice. . . . Having made every sacrifice of fortune and blood, and become a cripple in the service of my country, I little expected to meet the ungrateful returns I have received from my countrymen."

CHANGE OF HEART

While Arnold was reveling in his newfound prominence and respect, Peggy was throwing grand parties that helped to raise her husband's social profile—and his debts. The Arnolds enjoyed an extravagant lifestyle in Philadelphia, living well beyond their means, which may have contributed to Benedict's wandering eye in terms of his Patriotic allegiances.

Despite his initial zeal for taking up arms against the tyranny of King George, Arnold had long been losing faith in the Americans' chances at success, and the company he was keeping in Philadelphia did little to change his mind. Now it seemed he had his chance to throw in his lot with both sides and (if he played it right) emerge from the war a victor, no matter which army prevailed. In May 1779, Arnold made overtures to General Clinton in New York, by way of a Loyalist merchant in Philadelphia, as to whether he could be of service. The British did not immediately jump at his offer; after all, how often does a high-ranking enemy officer voluntarily offer to spy? Suspicions were rampant, but the proposal seemed legitimate and, if Arnold could prove himself trustworthy to the king, his intelligence would be an invaluable source of information about American strategies, plans, and plots. To test Arnold's proposal by degrees, Major John André, the newly appointed chief of intelligence for the British army, contacted Arnold—a connection aided, no doubt, by André's previous acquaintance with Arnold's new wife.

The correspondence between the two men often involved Peggy. Even as she acted as a messenger between Philadelphia girls and their British lovers who were now stationed in New York, secretly carrying letters and parcels back and forth, she would now also act as a courier between André's agent and her own husband. Her conduct on the first count was an open secret, which provided an excellent cover for her more nefarious role.

Arnold used a method similar to that of the Culpers when communicating with André: invisible ink and a book-based code. He based his code on two books: William Blackstone's *Commentaries on the Laws of England* and Nathan Bailey's *An Universal Etymological English Dictionary*. Each word was denoted by three numbers separated by a period. The first was the page number, the second was the line, and the third was the position of the word, starting from the left margin, in that line. For example, 172.8.7s stood for "troops": page 172, line 8, seventh word in. The *s* at the end simply made it plural. Like the communications of the Culpers and other spies of the era, the letters of Arnold and André were often disguised as ordinary notes about family matters or inconsequential gossip addressed to or written by Peggy. In between the lines, written in some form of invisible ink, were the real messages.

Despite the similarities in technique between the two spy rings, the Culpers were operating with several advantages. First, they had an added layer of security: Not every member or satellite was aware of the identities of the others in the ring. Arnold and André and their various go-betweens knew the names of everyone with whom they were dealing, which meant a higher risk of detection should someone be caught. Second, Arnold and André could communicate only with each other, but the Culpers had developed a more complex network that allowed Woodhull, Brewster, or Roe to add intelligence en route to General Washington, confirming or correcting the initial reports, and making the information more detailed when it finally reached its intended destination.

Third, the Culpers were able to operate in a wider social circle because the members were citizens from all walks of life. Townsend gathered information from soldiers around the city and sailors at the dock; Agent 355 charmed strategic details out of high-ranking officers at soirees; Rivington repeated gossip and plans overheard in his shop; Woodhull enhanced these reports with his own observations of troop activities on Long Island and recounted what shop owners were saying or if there was an uptick in lumber sales and ship repairs; Roe learned whatever news was shared when tongues loosened in his tavern; and from the water Brewster spied on British naval movements. The

Arnolds and André were limited to the upper tier of
Loyalist social circles for their intelligence.

EVERY MAN HAS HIS PRICE

Arnold's double-dealings had to be sidelined in the autumn of 1779 when suspicions fell on a number of Loyalists still residing and working in Philadelphia.
Because Arnold had married into one of the most
prominent Tory families, he, too, found himself forced
to prove his allegiance to the Continental Army and
the American cause.

Further complicating matters and frustrating Arnold was the fact that he faced a court-martial for some
of his business dealings in the city. Never mind that
the trial had initially been his idea when the concerns
were first raised; he had hoped that just such an event
would be an excellent opportunity to publicly shame
his critics and exonerate himself. Now, it just seemed
to add to his stress by bringing his actions under close
scrutiny—an uncomfortable prospect for anyone leading a double life.

The hearing went forward, however, and Arnold
conducted himself brilliantly. On January 26, 1780, he
was found guilty of two minor charges; the rest were
dropped. It was a tremendous moral victory for Arnold, and he wasted no time or expense in spreading
the word that he had prevailed over his detractors. To
make his happiness complete, six weeks later Peggy
gave birth to their first child, a boy named Edward

Shippen Arnold, after the baby's maternal grand-father.

The celebration was soon dampened, however, when the Continental Congress conducted a kind of self-audit and ruled in April that Arnold owed the government more than one thousand pounds for undocumented expenses from the unsuccessful invasion of Quebec he helped to lead in 1775. The records showed a substantial sum tied to Arnold for which there was no accounting or receipts; according to practice, the amount due was his own responsibility.

The investigation humiliated Arnold—and also put him in a financial bind. Shortly after the audit, he struck up a correspondence once again with the British. General Clinton was especially interested in expanding his grasp on New York beyond the boundaries of Long Island and Manhattan, and was eyeing the Hudson Valley as a means of controlling the land north of the Hudson River as well as the harbor. He would handsomely reward Arnold for his assistance, but Arnold and Peggy were still locked in Patriot Philadelphia, which wasn't nearly so rich a grounds for the intelligence Clinton and André desired. Despite his willingness to sell what he knew, the damage that Arnold was able to inflict upon the American cause was somewhat limited by his current capacity and location. Clinton wanted to see his spy situated somewhere much more significant for the Crown's goals of reestablishing authority over as much land, population, and key transportation and resource channels as possible, and he urged Arnold to seek new opportunities and a new command.

For the past year, Arnold had found life in Philadelphia quite to his liking, but now he was fed up. The bill from Congress for the invasion of Quebec was as humiliating as it was beyond his ability to pay. He had heard that the command at Fort West Point was available, and it seemed the perfect solution to his various woes. While he may not have relished the thought of moving to a remote outpost, the thought of being in absolute authority in his own fort away from Philadelphia must have appealed to his pride. He could quit the city, assume control of the strategic fort, and at precisely the right time turn it over to the British. He would then collect his reward and enjoy a life of leisure as the man who had made the king's victory over the rebellion possible. Away in New York, General Clinton, too, recognized the potential of West Point; it was situated fifty-five miles north of Manhattan, on a sharp turn of the Hudson River. From there, it was possible to control the access of ships to the rest of the river, thereby limiting or opening the movement of troops, supplies, and goods for trade. It was, in many ways, the key to the rest of the state. Through Major André, he urged Arnold to press his case for the command of the fort.

Washington resisted the petition at first. Arnold had resigned his position in Philadelphia after the Quebec payment insult, and despite his acquittal on all but two minor charges resulting from the court-martial, his conduct in those matters had still been disappointing. Washington had personally written a strongly worded letter to Arnold chastising him for such behavior not long after the verdict was handed down, despite which Arnold had commenced with his very public celebrations of the outcome. Still, West Point needed an experienced man at its helm, and much of Arnold's combat and strategy experience had been in upstate New York. Washington mulled over the matter even as Arnold and several of his allies lobbied heavily for the appointment.

With a permanent departure from Philadelphia on his mind, Arnold set off for New Haven in order to settle his affairs in that city, as well as to begin quietly transferring his cash assets to London banks. He deliberately routed his travels so that he could stop and inspect West Point on the way under the guise of wanting to get a sense of the state of the fort to better prepare for taking command. He secretly sent off whatever information he was able to gather to André with the implied promise that much more would follow should their plan succeed and he be given control in the coming months. Initially, the price he named for his treachery was ten thousand pounds, in addition to his out-of-pocket costs and losses (which makes Woodhull's occasional requests to General Washington for fifty pounds to reimburse members of the Culper Ring seem humble, paltry, even laughable). But Arnold knew the British had the money and he was certain they would pay as much for the information as for the sheer satisfaction of humiliating the Americans.

Just a few weeks later, however, whether from

discovering that his debts in Connecticut were far worse than he had anticipated, from finding Peggy's influence greatly diminished with his geographical separation from her, or simply from losing heart, Arnold suddenly grew panicked, even paranoid. In a letter to André dated July 11, 1780, he complained that he was not being trusted and hinted that he would put a stop to the whole deal unless things changed to his satisfaction. The next day, he wrote again, this time doubling his price to twenty thousand pounds, overtly offering to surrender the fort, and insisting that a portion of the reward be tendered as a down payment for his services.

In all fairness, Arnold's anxiety was not unfounded. He was, in fact, being spied upon by order of General Clinton because the British did not consider him altogether trustworthy; after all, if he changed his loyalties once, what was to stop him from playing the turncoat again? But his course was set and he was determined to carry it out, certain that he would emerge as victor in the end.

CHAPTER 12

Negotiations and Treachery

Benedict Arnold's treason was well under way when the French fleet arrived in Newport during the summer of 1780. Observing that Washington was actively working on several covert plans to outmaneuver the British, Arnold tried just as actively to undo them in secret. Fortunately for Washington, the deep secrecy surrounding the Culpers kept the ring out of Arnold's reach, but the success of the spies' tip and Washington's ruse had alerted Benedict Arnold. He knew he would need to infiltrate or stop the ring were his betrayal to be successful. Little did he know that members of the very ring he was attempting to ensnare were removed from him by just a few degrees of separation.

At the end of July, with the French troops safely disembarked in Rhode Island, Washington prepared to ride out to meet them and proposed that Arnold lead a raid against some of Clinton's troops stationed around New York at the same time. Arnold pleaded to be excused from such exertion, using the same reasoning he had back in March to remove himself from other action: An injury had left him with a stiff ankle, and his doctors had recommended that he not take command of an army until it healed. Conceding to Arnold's requests and complaints, Washington kept him off the battlefield and diverted him instead to the less physically demanding post as commander of West Point, exactly as Arnold had hoped. On August 3, 1780, Benedict Arnold found himself the most powerful man on the Hudson.

He wasted no time in capitalizing on his new position. Almost immediately he began repairing the fort and stocking it with as many provisions as possible. If he was going to turn West Point over to the British, he might as well win points with his new commanders by outfitting it on the American dime first; he even consulted a French engineer fighting alongside the Americans, Major Chevalier de Villefranche. "Major Villefranche has surveyed the works at West Point, and informs me that there is a vast deal to do to complete them," Arnold wrote Washington on August 8. "That large quantities of materials, such as timber, plank, boards, stone, &c., will be wanted. Part of the materials are at different places near this post; but I do not find that there are any teams or forage in the department, and, at present there is no prospect of any being furnished."

Even more urgently, Arnold began to inquire about the names and addresses of Patriot spies he claimed might be of importance to him in defending the fort against any planned attacks by the British. Of particular interest to Arnold was the ring operating in New

York, upon whom Washington had relied so heavily in the recent incident with the French fleet as well as in previous matters of significant intelligence, such as troop movements on Long Island and the foiled counterfeiting plan. The commander in chief declined the request out of both honor and necessity; he did not know the identity of most of his spies by design and he had sworn to uphold the secrecy of those he did know. Lafayette responded to Arnold's request in a similar manner.

Disappointed that he was not able to ensnare the Culpers, which would have delighted General Clinton no end, Arnold nevertheless pursued whatever prey he could. On August 5, Arnold wrote a letter to Major General Robert Howe of the Continental Army, begging for this same information about a few operatives in Howe's employ in such an eloquent and reasonable manner that his motives seemed quite aboveboard. "As the safety of this Post and garrison in a great measure depends on having good intelligence of the movements and designs of the enemy," he penned, "and as you have been fortunate in the agents you have employed for that purpose, I must request, with their permission, to be informed who they are, as I wish to employ them, for the same purpose. I will engage upon them to make no discovery of them to any person breathing."

Howe replied nine days later in a manner that shows he was clearly distressed by his spies' response at the time, though it must have seemed a tremendous blessing only a few weeks later when Arnold's true nature was revealed:

The two most intelligent and confidential I got to undertake with difficulty, and they did it with the greatest reluctance and not without my pledging in the most solemn manner my honor not to inform any person upon earth of their names, or of their acting in the capacity of emisarys, they are persons of character and property, who cannot without utter ruin get out of the enemy's power, and yet devoted to America, have agreed to serve in a way they do not like, but which is the only way they can at present serve her in. I have written to them and urged them to let me give their address to you, but . . . they in the most positive terms refused; and it is not without great persuasion and difficulty that they are prevailed upon to continue their acting even for me; this makes me fear they will not consent to it tho I sincerely wish they may. I cannot indeed blame this caution, as their life and the ruin of their families must be the certain consequence should any accident happen to them.

Howe did manage to persuade one operative in his employ to correspond with Arnold, though this was under an assumed name. "He will mark the letters Private, and you must injoin your family not to open any letters so marked," Howe warned in the closing of his message.

Arnold's response was gracious, if disappointed. He had clearly anticipated obtaining specific details about the various covert operatives at work in and around New York that he could pass on to André via Peggy, but had learned almost nothing. He pledged his honor to Howe that he would not expose the one man who had agreed to send information to Arnold, nor reveal his name should he accidentally discover it. In a culture where a man's honor was considered quite sacred, these sentiments seem especially crass given Arnold's intention, but, to his credit, he was not entirely disingenuous. "I will take proper precautions that no gentlemen of my family open any letters addressed to me as Private," he added. Peggy, after all, was not a gentleman.

A WOLF IN SILK AND LACE

Peggy Arnold was not the only woman with a secret connected to Benedict Arnold. The whirl of celebration that had died down with the absence of the British top brass from New York now began anew, and Agent 355 found herself once again in the company of New York's wealthiest Loyalists and most powerful British officers. The gossip was generally unchanged. Many of the well-to-do families of the Northeast were casually connected through intermarriage or business associations of one kind or another. More than one family loyal to King George had a cousin or two serving under General George Washington, nor was it unheard of that a family with one political allegiance should suddenly find itself related to one of the opposite persuasion when members from each decided to wed.

Therefore, it didn't seem unusual at all that the Arnolds' names should come up in conversation that summer. Benedict's family was established just across the border in Connecticut, and the former Miss Shippen—whose own family was extremely well connected—had been acquainted with many of the officers now in New York. Benedict Arnold's name might have even been something of a joke, at first, among the British. Here was an overly eager merchant–turned–major general who seemed desperate for praise and for cash—and was willing to go to great lengths for either one. His price changed even as his emotional investment did, and his letters were at once full of self-importance and a kind of panicked need for validation. The officers who despised him may have ridiculed him over their drinks within 355's hearing.

By September, however, the snickering would have ceased. Arnold had assumed the command he and General Clinton had both so desperately wanted for him, and no time had been wasted in accepting his terms of surrender. Only a few things were needed now to bring the whole plan to fruition. First, an opportunity to familiarize the British with the plans of the fort so that they could exploit its vulnerabilities and storm it as swiftly as possible and, second, time to get the necessary men and weapons in place to ensure that any resistance the Patriots offered was futile.

No plans of such a sensitive nature were explicitly discussed in social settings like dinner parties, but certain phrases, pointed glances, and delicious insinuations that something was coming would have abounded among the most senior officers. Red-faced brass chortled, slapping each other on the back and toasting their port glasses to the Hudson River or to West Point itself.

When Major André let drop in conversation that he was going north for a few days, anyone who was simply mingling for company, conversation, and culinary delights would have assumed he was attending to routine business. To someone with a more serious mission than simply seeing and being seen, however, something seemed amiss in these veiled hints. What exactly was afoot was unclear, but the lady whose job it was to "out wit them all" would have reported what she had observed.

TWO WOLVES IN MERCHANTS' SHIRTSLEEVES

While his name was being bandied around New York's most exclusive circles during his first weeks of command, Arnold was quite busy sending letters. Besides writing to Washington about his desire to increase the provisions and make improvements at the fort and composing letters about his need to learn the identity of spies, Arnold also found the time to send a letter to an American outpost, informing its members that a certain merchant from the city by the name of John Anderson might be passing their way and begging their assistance in helping him to secure safe passage to West Point. Additionally, Arnold was also carrying on his correspondence with André so as to arrange the meeting outside the city that would finalize their negotiations and plans for the handing over of the fort.

When the long-anticipated meeting finally took place, André was to pose as a prosperous businessman, Arnold as his patron. In keeping with their cover, the men wrote their letters not in the numbered code or invisible ink of their previous exchanges, but very much in the role of a client and a vendor making plans to carry out a large transaction—which, in many ways, they were, though the roles were reversed.

Townsend, meanwhile, found that when he left his shop to observe the goings-on around Manhattan that September he could not help but notice the uptick in preparations along the docks. The British were clearly fitting ships for some kind of engagement, though Townsend could not be sure if this was merely a response to the arrival of the French fleet and the fear that a naval battle might be brewing, or if it was with some other specific aim. Even the soldiers and sailors with whom he conversed seemed uncertain as to their orders. It seemed unlikely that significant troop movements would be following so closely on the heels of the intentional misinformation regarding Washington's supposed plans to attack the city and the unanticipated recall of troops. Then again, the blow to Clinton's pride that incident had delivered may have prompted him to plan an aggressive response simply to prove he would not be made the fool.

The increase of activity in mid-September was definitely new, though, after a relatively quiet August. Woodhull had written to Tallmadge on September 1: "In regard of the state of affairs in general he [Culper Junior] assured the express they remained as heretofore or as when wrote you last, nothing new, everything appeared to be at a stand, and the enemy much embarissed expecting an attack." Despite the calm in the city in August, troops had continued to shift around Long Island, and Woodhull had even mentioned that a British spy had crossed the Sound to Connecticut—a man who was "positively an agent for the enemy. He hath been a long time serviceable in that way, and this is his second embassy. I know it to be true and have lately had a perfect knowledge of his conduct for this three years past, and have been solicited by his friend as an assistant."

It was worth noting, but hardly earthshaking news. Spies were everywhere, and both sides knew it. That this operative tried to convert Woodhull to his side while clearly unaware as to Woodhull's true loyalties is both comical and a testimony to the convincing role Woodhull was playing as a man of profound apathy. His secret letters, however, reveal just how deep his passions truly ran. Four days later, Woodhull wrote again to Tallmadge to inform him of a movement of troops away from Setauket, which left the town much more vulnerable to an American invasion to reclaim it: "For God's sake attack them, you'll certainly be successful, if you are secret about it. . . . Setauket is exceedingly distressed. Pray offer some relief."

No prospect could have delighted Tallmadge more than the possibility of liberating his hometown, and he wrote to Washington to propose just such a raid: "The enclosed Dispatches from Culper have this moment come to hand. . . . C. writes with great sollicitude for troops to be sent from this side to attack those lying at Setauket. I need not repeat to your Excellency how exceedingly happy I should be to assist in such an

Expedition, should it be thot. advisable." To Tall-madge's disappointment, Washington did not approve the plan, and he would have to wait several more months before he could wage battle on Long Island.

As the warm weather faded, Townsend continued to submit reports written in invisible ink, which now fell almost exclusively on Tallmadge to reveal and decipher. The job had previously belonged to Washington's aide-de-camp Alexander Hamilton, while Tallmadge was in charge of making sense of the general intelligence and summary reports Woodhull, Roe, and Brewster compiled. But recently Tallmadge had been tasked with the white-ink letters—perhaps after Washington recog-nized the urgency of the information conveyed about the French troops—and Tallmadge found himself even more impressed now with the quality and accuracy of Townsend's reports than he had been before.

None of them knew, however, just quite what they were in the midst of in September 1780. The reports from the city, the strange behaviors, the activity with the ships—Tallmadge couldn't put his finger on it, but his instincts told him something was not right. He felt as if he had nearly all the elements in front of him, al-most all the clues gathered, but he was not sure what he was looking at or what the picture was that he needed to assemble. That he had letters on his desk from his merchant-spy in New York regarding an officer from New York venturing toward West Point seemed wholly unconnected. Despite all the hints he received from 355, Woodhull, and Townsend, Tallmadge didn't con-nect the dots until it was almost too late.

CHAPTER 13

The Deal Is Done

On the afternoon of Sunday, September 10, 1780, Benedict Arnold stepped onto a barge under the auspices of meeting with his long-awaited merchant friend from New York, John Anderson. If the general seemed nervous or anxious, the bargemen took no notice. They, too, were probably on alert for British gunboats patrolling the waters of the lower Hudson River and were not especially delighted with the thought of traveling southward toward enemy territory. They followed the river several miles, then let Arnold off on the shore to stay the night at the home of a friend who lived near the river. The next morning, the crew sailed the approximately twenty miles remaining to Dobbs Ferry, where the meeting was to take place.

As the barge approached, a barrage of British gunfire opened up on the little vessel, which quickly retreated upriver a safe distance. Arnold, who had not anticipated this attack, ordered the crew to land the barge on the west bank of the river, where he could safely await Anderson's arrival at a small outpost of American troops. The merchant never appeared, and Arnold, forced to declare the meeting a failure, returned to West Point. André, it turns out, had been in the vicinity, but the vigilant gunboats had made crossing the river quite perilous in risking both his life and recognition by some of his own soldiers. He returned to New York to arrange a second attempt at meeting with his coconspirator.

Colonel Simcoe, the cold-blooded leader of the Queen's Rangers who had occupied the Townsend Homestead in Oyster Bay, had some time past been ransomed from his prison in New Jersey and was once again commanding his men on raids. André had promised him the privilege of being present for the surrender of the fort, but Simcoe now received word that the rangers were being ordered to ride south toward Chesapeake Bay and wrote to André greatly worried that this sudden change would cause him to miss out on the fun. "Rely upon it your alarms are vain," André wrote the day after his missed rendezvous with Arnold. He added, tantalizingly, "I should have been happy to have seen you and have hinted that apparent arrangements are not always real ones, but I beg you to seek no explanation."

On September 15, Arnold penned a letter to "John Anderson" recounting the failed meeting and attempting to set up another opportunity "on Wednesday the 20th instant" at the same location. ("Instant" was a form of eighteenth-century shorthand meaning "of the current month.") He may have regarded their missing each other as a bad omen, and was certainly feeling agitated and exposed. "The foregoing letter was written to caution you not to mention your business to Colonel Sheldon, or any other person," he warned, clearly concerned that André might play his part as a Patriot merchant too convincingly by chatting with the leader of the Light Dragoons as he passed through their patrol area. "I have no confidant. I have made one too many already." The letter, which he signed "Gustavus" as he had several of this series of messages, was directed toward New York, and Arnold returned his attention to making his preparations.

He had been quite eager to learn the itinerary of General Washington, a fact that Alexander Hamilton later noted may have been an attempt to secure the commander in chief's capture along with the fort. In fact, Arnold's letters indicate that he was anticipating Washington's arrival at West Point in a matter of days with the intent of the general's staying Saturday night at the fort. The main focus of the plan, however, was to secure the handover; Arnold, after all, was acting more from a sense of monetary gain than from any deep-seated political zeal regarding who would ultimately win the conflict.

JOHN ANDERSON SETS FORTH

The evening of Monday, September 18, witnessed an elaborate dinner party at the home of a well-to-do New York Loyalist. Though it was hosted in honor of

General Clinton and his closest officers, special attention was paid to Major André, and it seems to actually have been something of an unofficial send-off for the young man, as he was about to embark upon a mission that, they hoped, would result in one of the greatest victories for the British since the war began.

The next day André set out northward with the goal of reaching HMS *Vulture,* a fourteen-gun sloop docked near Teller's Point, by evening. Because it was a British ship, he arrived not as "John Anderson, Patriot merchant" but as himself, bearing letters from General Clinton that needed to be hand-delivered farther up-country. The crew was ignorant as to the true nature of André's visit, likely because of their proximity to West Point. Should any sailor let a casual word slip while onshore, the whole deal would be ruined. André boarded the *Vulture* for the night and awaited a message from Arnold for their meeting the next day. None came.

On Thursday, September 21, Arnold received a letter complaining that boats from West Point had fired upon a small vessel traveling to shore under the flag of truce, which was a violation of the terms of war. "Fortunately none of my people were hurt, but the treacherous intentions of those who fired are not vindicated from that circumstance," Captain Sutherland had written. The note was signed by both the captain and a certain "John Anderson." André's likely explanation to Sutherland for the pseudonym was that they could expect an attack should the Americans know

that André himself was currently on board; the real
reason, of course, was to alert Arnold to his presence
on the ship.

André also wrote a letter back to his command,
stating:

> *As the tide was favorable on my arrival at the*
> *sloop yesterday, I determined to be myself the*
> *bearer of your Excellency's letters as far as the Vul-*
> *ture. I have suffered for it, having caught a very*
> *bad cold, and had so violent a return of a disorder*
> *in my stomach which had attacked me a few days*
> *ago, that Captain Sutherland and Colonel Robin-*
> *son [Beverly Robinson, at whose home Arnold was*
> *staying] insist on my remaining on board till I am*
> *better. I hope tomorrow to get down again.*

He also included a private message intended just
for General Clinton's eyes: "Nobody has appeared.
This is the second expedition I have made without an
ostensible reason, and Col. Robinson both times of the
party. A third would infallibly fire suspicions. I have
therefore thought it best to remain here on plea of sick-
ness, as my enclosed letter will feign, and try further
expedients."

That same night, Arnold ordered some boatmen to
row to the *Vulture* under a flag of truce, and to bring
back with them a certain gentleman on board. Arnold
could not approach the *Vulture* himself without arous-
ing suspicion, given his rank and current assignment.

In his stead, he sent Joshua Hett Smith, a local resident whom he charged with managing the retrieval. One of the rowers, a seasoned old hand, complained when ordered to muffle the oars to disguise their sound, lest a patrol boat find them. "If the business is of a fair and upright nature, as you assure us it is, I see no necessity for any disguise or to seize the veil of night to execute what might be as well transacted in broad daylight," he grumbled to the general.

Arnold responded by ordering the crew to carry out their plans as he had charged them, coolly reminding them, "I have the command of the militia of the county for sixty miles around West Point by the order of Congress."

The party set out with no further objections and approached the *Vulture* with the truce flag hoisted. Smith climbed aboard and, after explaining his task and showing his passes to the officers in charge, Anderson was introduced and agreed to accompany Smith back to shore for the meeting. "Very little conversation passed between Mr. Anderson and myself," Smith later recalled, "excepting trivial remarks about the tide, the weather, and matters of no concern. Mr. Anderson, from his youthful appearance and the softness of his manners, did not seem to me to be qualified for a business of such moment." But Smith conveyed him back to shore anyway, trusting that General Arnold knew best.

After introducing the two men—both of whom were dressed in blue coats—Smith was ordered to return to the boat to wait with the crew. This annoyed him somewhat, as he felt he had earned the right to be present for the discussion, given his efforts in bringing the meeting about, but he did as he was told. Some time later, Arnold and his friend returned and the order was given to bring Anderson back to the *Vulture,* but Smith objected. The men were tired and could not possibly make the trip back to the ship and to shore once again before sunrise, when they were sure to be spotted. He proposed that if the cover of darkness was, indeed, so very important to Arnold that they had best wait until the following evening to venture out again. Arnold conceded the point and Smith opened his home to them for the remainder of the night.

By morning, it was clear that the rowboat would have had an even more strenuous voyage than previously anticipated. The *Vulture* was sailing southward, having been fired upon by American guns. André was very anxious about the situation because the longer he remained off the ship and in American territory, the greater his risk of capture. Arnold persuaded him to take advantage of the day, however, and the two rode out, presumably to inspect some of the routes to West Point and plan for the best possible approach by foot soldiers supplementing the attack from the river.

But as evening drew near, it was evident that André would have no hope of sailing back to New York on the damaged *Vulture* and would need to return to the city by land instead. "I wish I was on board," he said with a heavy sigh, looking in the direction of the ship, but he set out toward White Plains on horseback with

Smith and a servant accompanying him for the first part of the journey to help him navigate the unfamiliar territory. Smith stopped at several waypoints to converse with the Patriot soldiers stationed along the route, but André kept to himself so that witnesses later recalled little other than that a man with a round, floppy hat and cape fastened tightly around his neck was a member of the riding party. Smith was well known to many of the American militiamen in the area and respected among them because, as one man later noted, "I had heard it frequently mentioned that [American] General [Robert] Howe used to employ Mr. Smith in getting intelligence." Other American officers held Smith in contempt; at least one suspected him of being a double agent and a few weeks prior had challenged Arnold on his association with the man.

Whatever the nature of Smith's character and his later claimed ignorance, he guided André easily through the American territory. Some of the men advised Smith against riding any farther that night, given the patrols in the area. Even if friendly, they might give him some trouble before checking for his pass signed by Arnold granting him safe passage; however, the militiamen were most concerned about the Cow Boys, a group of British marauders who made criminal mischief for residents in the area, stealing food supplies or robbing travelers. André would have been quite safe in their company, had they known his true identity—but he could not reveal himself as a British officer without tipping off Smith to the whole business. Reluctantly, André agreed that they should find shelter and resume their travels by daylight. Securing lodging at a nearby house, the men retired to rest, but, as Smith noted, "I was often disturbed with the restless motions, and uneasiness of mind exhibited by my bed-fellow, who on observing the first approach of day, summoned my servant to prepare the horses for our departure."

As the three men neared the bridge over the Croton River, which feeds into the Hudson River and provided the swiftest means through the remainder of the American territory back into the British-held districts approaching New York City, a profound change came over André. Shedding his anxiety and gloom, he began to be much more like the charming, cheerful wit so beloved by his comrades. "He appeared in the morning as if he had not slept an hour during the night; he at first was much dejected, but a pleasing change took place in his countenance when summoned to mount his horse," Smith remembered.

> I observed that the nearer we approached the bridge, the more his countenance brightened into a cheerful serenity, and he became very affable; in short, I now found him highly entertaining. . . . He descanted on the richness of the scenery around us, and particularly admired, from every eminence, the grandeur of the Highland mountains, bathing their summits in the clouds from their seeming watery base at the north extremity of Haverstraw Bay. The pleasantry of converse, and mildness of the weather, so insensibly

*beguiled the time that we at length found our-
selves at the bridge before I thought we had got
half way; and I now had reason to think my
fellow-traveller a very different person from the
character I had at first formed of him.*

André seemed quite touched by the well-intentioned
company of Smith and his servant, and as he prepared to
cross over the river and leave his new friends to head
home, he promised to return the saddle and bridle that
he had borrowed from Smith or send payment for them,
and he made an offer of "a valuable gold watch in remembrance of him, as a keep sake, which I refused." And
with that final gesture of generosity and amiability, André directed his horse over the bridge in the direction of
what he hoped would be a safe passage back to the city.

BETRAYAL IN BOOTS

On that same morning of September 23, three American militiamen, John Paulding, Isaac Van Wart, and
David Williams, were guarding the road in a kind of
no-man's-land en route to the city. So far, the watch
had been dull, with only familiar local faces passing
by. But when they spotted a stranger making his way
down the road, one of the members of the party whispered, "There comes a gentleman-like looking man,
who appears to be well dressed, and has boots on,
who you had better step out and stop if you don't
know him."

Paulding stepped forward and raised his firelock at the stranger. "Stand!" he demanded. "Where are you going?"

"I am a British officer out of the country, on particular business, and I hope you won't detain me a minute!" André said, flashing the gold watch he had previously offered to Smith either to make a play on words or else to prove his claim, as only a high-ranking gentleman could afford such a timepiece.

"Dismount," Paulding ordered, not amused.

"My God, I must do anything to get 'along,'" he said, laughing and pulling out the pass from General Benedict Arnold that granted him safe passage. Then, climbing down from the horse, he replied more seriously, "Gentlemen you had best let me go, or you will bring yourselves in trouble, for, by your stopping of me you will detain the General's business. I'm to go to Dobb's Ferry to meet a person there."

It was a difficult situation for the three men. Did they dare hold up a man with a pass from a general in order to search him? Did they dare not to?

Finally, Paulding spoke again. "I hope you will not be offended. There are many bad people going along the road, and I do not know but perhaps you might be one. Have you any letters about you?"

André replied coolly, "No."

Sensing something was amiss, the men searched his clothes but found nothing hidden. Then Paulding ordered André to remove his boots. He removed one rather reluctantly and in a slightly awkward manner.

Rather than feel around in the boot itself, Paulding reached out and grasped André's foot, where he felt paper in his stocking. "Pull off the other boot," Paulding ordered. With three firearms pointed at his head, André had no choice but to comply. Paulding regarded the papers briefly, then announced to Van Wart and Williams, "This is a spy."

Williams winked at his friends. "What would you give us to let you go?"

"Any sum of money."

"Would you give us your horse, saddle, bridle, watch—and a hundred guineas?"

"Yes," André responded. "I will direct it to any place even if it is to this very spot, so that you can get it."

"Would you give us more?" Williams goaded, clearly enjoying the gentleman's distress.

"I'll give you any quantity of dry goods or any sum of money, and bring it to any place you might pitch upon so that you might get it."

"No, by God!" Paulding roared. "If you would give us ten thousand guineas, you should not stir a step."

The three militiamen marched their prisoner to a nearby American camp at North Castle to turn him over to Lieutenant Colonel John Jameson. Along the way, the younger two men questioned him, still not clear as to his identity but hoping to have a little fun at his expense. André's sophisticated sensibilities finally had enough of the backwoods banter. "I beg you would ask me none till we come to some officers and then I will reveal the whole," he pleaded. He was turned over to Jameson's custody, and the three militiamen went on their way to resume guarding the road.

JAMESON'S MISTAKE

Colonel Jameson was mortified by the situation in which he now found himself. Three overeager men had just delivered to his camp a man bearing a pass from General Arnold; perhaps they were so excited at the prospect of having captured a British officer that they were blind to the fact that the pass should have automatically granted him safe passage, no questions asked—certainly arrest or detention was not necessary.

The commandeered papers had been forwarded on for Washington's inspection—rushed on Jameson's special orders—but now Jameson was faced with the matter of what to do with the man currently in his custody. He certainly spoke like a rational, genteel man, not a panicked spy caught in a snare, and his simple request was to be escorted back to West Point, where General Arnold would explain everything and set the matter straight. It seemed logical to Jameson, so he hurried to make the arrangements to carry it out, lest he find himself on the receiving end of one of Arnold's infamous angry outbursts.

Benjamin Tallmadge, meanwhile, had just returned to North Castle that evening from a daylong scouting mission. He heard talk of the newly apprehended prisoner named John Anderson brought in that morning; something seemed strange about the

story but so much had of late that it was hard to pin-
point what was so unsettling. As Tallmadge sat re-
viewing the letters that had accumulated in his
absence, as well as those he had put aside before he
left, he happened to spot a note from General Arnold
sent some days previous, informing him of a certain
man named John Anderson who might pass Tallmadge's way: "I have to request that you will give him
an escort of two Horse to bring him on this way to this
place, and send an express to me that I may meet him."
Suddenly, it all made sense—the prisoner, the strange
reports he was receiving from the Culpers in New
York, and Arnold's odd behavior.

Tallmadge rushed to Jameson and demanded to
see the prisoner, but the colonel informed him it was
impossible: John Anderson was gone from North Castle on Jameson's orders, escorted by a lieutenant with a
letter explaining the situation, through the open country back to General Arnold at West Point.

CHAPTER 14

Another Spy at the Gallows

Major Benjamin Tallmadge respected the chain of command and he respected his senior officers, but in this instance he knew that his commanding officer had made a perilous mistake. Colonel Jameson had sensed that something was amiss, because he had rushed the papers found on the prisoner to Washington for examination, but fear of displeasing Arnold had clouded his better judgment, prompting him to return the prisoner to Arnold as he requested. Chagrined, Jameson was willing to listen to his subordinate's suggestions.

Tallmadge was a spymaster and much more savvy about the backhanded operations of intelligence gathering than Jameson. Hearing a full account of the story, he recognized the seemingly disparate pieces and concluded that a major betrayal was at hand. His first thought was to suggest a daring mission designed to entrap all the involved parties. He proposed the scheme to Jameson, who found the plan much too bold. Tallmadge later wrote to a friend and historian: "[I] did not fail to state the glaring inconsistency of their conduct to Lt. Col. Jameson in a private and most friendly manner. He appeared greatly agitated, more especially when I suggested to him a plan which I wished to pursue, offering to take the entire responsibility on myself, and which, as he deemed it too perilous to permit, I will not further disclose."

With his first suggestion rejected, Tallmadge immediately pursued the next best way of intercepting the prisoner and returning him to their custody. Jameson remained hesitant, afraid of upsetting General Arnold, but Tallmadge finally managed to persuade him to rescind his order and bring André back to North Castle while they awaited word from Washington. Oddly enough, Jameson still insisted on informing Arnold of the turn of events. "Strange as it may seem," Tallmadge wrote, "Lt. Col. J. would persist in his purpose of sending his letter to Gen. Arnold—The letter did go on, and was the first information that Arch Traitor received that his plot was blown up. The Officer returned [to Jameson's camp] with his prisoner early the next morning."

Jameson's decision to alert Arnold to the matter, while shocking in retrospect, was quite understandable, given Arnold's reputation. For one thing, Arnold was widely trusted by many officers of the Continental Army; even those who held him in contempt would generally not have anticipated that his imprudence could go so far as to commit treason. Tallmadge noted later that Jameson, in writing to Arnold about the matter, "expressed great confidence in him as I believe was the case thro' the army. Until the papers were found on Anderson, I had no suspicion of his lack of patriotism or political integrity." For another, Arnold was widely feared, and Jameson was willing to take extreme steps to protect himself from the man's wrath for not following his directives. Had Tallmadge not been as acutely attuned to subtle clues and not been actively trying to piece together the Culper Ring's reports, he, too, might have fallen under Arnold's spell and failed to realize who John Anderson was.

Even now, Tallmadge kept the spies in mind and realized that more than just the fate of Fort West Point was at stake. The surrender of the fort had to be stopped at all costs, but in a somewhat delicate way. André would not have broadcast his travel plans beyond a select circle, and the collapse of his plan could endanger the spies who had helped unravel the plot. If word reached the British that there was a mole in André's inner circle, Agent 355 and any of her associates— like Townsend—could be quickly unmasked. The entire ring would collapse, and the gallows would become a little more crowded. Tallmadge would have to act swiftly but carefully.

THE PRIZE OF WEST POINT

General Washington was riding toward West Point on the evening of Sunday, September 24. He had been visiting Hartford, Connecticut, and his schedule had changed slightly from his original plan to arrive on Saturday. Still, he imagined Arnold would be happy to see him, just as he was eager to see what improvements Arnold had put into effect at the fort, now that he had been in command nearly two months.

Washington intended to arrive late that evening but found himself detained out of politeness with a friend, and decided to lodge at a nearby inn for the night and finish his journey in the morning. Very early the next day, Washington sent Alexander Hamilton ahead with the baggage for the last fifteen miles to announce their arrival to Arnold and suggest that Washington breakfast with him before touring the fort.

To Washington's surprise, when he arrived at West Point not long after Hamilton, Arnold was not waiting for him. Instead, as Washington would later recall:

> *Soon after he [Hamilton] arrived at Arnold's headquarters, a letter was delivered to Arnold which threw him into the greatest confusion. He told Colonel Hamilton that something required his immediate attendance at the garrison which was on the opposite side of the river to his quarters; and immediately ordered a horse, to take him to the river; and the barge which he kept to cross, to be ready; and desired Major Franks, his Aid, to inform me when I should arrive that he was gone over the river and would return immediately.*

It was a strange reception for his commander in chief, but Arnold was, admittedly, something of a strange man. Washington decided not to stand on ceremony, but simply went about his day as he would have had Arnold been present as planned. He had breakfast, then rode down to the river to view the fortifications of the garrison and anticipated, not unreasonably, that he would encounter Arnold in the process. When Arnold still failed to materialize, however, Washington began to ask the men standing guard where their commander was; none could tell him. Washington was puzzled. "The impropriety of his conduct when he knew I was to be there, struck me very forcibly, and my mind misgave me; but I had not the least idea of the real cause," he remembered.

After about two hours of inspecting the fort and inquiring after its officer in charge, Washington returned to Arnold's headquarters, where Hamilton was waiting with a parcel that had just arrived. The courier seemed in great concern that General Washington review the contents of the package immediately, as he had been traveling hard many hours to find him, under the strict orders that he should "ride night and day" until he reached the general. Having headed straight for Connecticut using the same route Washington had taken to get there, the unfortunate courier did not realize that Washington had taken a different road back. Thus, the rider had been frantically chasing the general from New York to Connecticut and back again in order to deliver the papers he carried, freshly plucked from the boot of a man going by the name of John Anderson.

Something was terribly, terribly wrong: First Arnold's absence and now this? Washington felt his concern grow as he reached for the packet, which explained the whole matter. Alarmed, Washington ordered Hamilton to mount his horse and gallop to a post on the river about eight miles below, hoping he could stop Arnold's barge. Hamilton pushed his horse to its limit, but he was too late. Benedict Arnold had escaped.

ARNOLD'S ESCAPE

When Alexander Hamilton had ridden up to the gates of West Point that morning, Arnold knew that General Washington would be following just an hour or two behind. He had been anticipating this visit for several days, though it is impossible to guess what Arnold's feelings might have been now that the commander in chief was about to enter through the very gates Arnold planned to swing open to the enemy upon their approach. For all he knew, André had made it safely back to New York and the British had a small fleet of ships sailing up the Hudson and several regiments of soldiers marching through the New York forests even now to storm the fort. If everything had gone according to plan—and Arnold had no reason to think it had not—the entire course of the war might be changed by the end of the day.

Arnold had little time to mull over his plan, because a lieutenant arrived very shortly after Hamilton, carrying a letter from Lieutenant Colonel Jameson explaining that a gentleman by the name of Anderson who was carrying passes issued by Arnold had been captured and had now been returned to confinement while some odd papers and plans found on him were sent to Washington via an express rider. It was all a wicked plan by the British, Jameson concluded, to besmirch Benedict Arnold's good name and to cause division in the ranks by undermining the Continental Army's confidence in him. He just felt Arnold should be made aware of the slanderous efforts being made against him by the enemy.

The jig was up. Arnold's worst fears had all been realized: The Americans were aware (or soon would be) of the depth of his treachery, but the British had yet to do anything to capture the fort and, without the plans, likely never would be able to do so. Thus, he was a traitor to one group, but hardly the hero he had anticipated becoming to the other. Now he would be nothing more than a failed turncoat—if he was even able to escape with his life, that is.

Making hasty apologies to Hamilton and to his own aide, who were both waiting for Washington's arrival and the tour to begin, Arnold dashed off toward the water full of empty promises to return promptly, just as soon as he sorted out some urgent matter across the river. He called for his bargemen to row him as swiftly as possible downstream toward where HMS *Vulture* had recently retreated, explaining to the confused men at the oars that they would receive two gallons of rum apiece if they did their job quickly, as he would need to turn around very shortly to meet General Washington for his much anticipated visit. They exerted themselves admirably. The barge reached the *Vulture* under a flag of truce, which kept them from being fired upon and allowed Arnold to board in safety. His loyal crew was also taken aboard, where Arnold promptly informed them that they were now prisoners of the British army.

Peggy and baby Edward, meanwhile, were left behind at West Point—entrusted to what Arnold knew would be the merciful and benevolent judgment of General Washington.

ANDRÉ'S FATE

After being intercepted on his way to West Point, John André (whose true identity was not yet known by his captors) was taken to Salem, Connecticut, where Colonel Elisha Sheldon, commanding officer of Tallmadge's own Second Light Dragoons, was headquartered. André seemed to have given Jameson little trouble, but upon being transferred to Sheldon's supervision at Salem on September 24, Tallmadge noted that "it was manifest that his agitation and anxiety increased."

Later that afternoon, André made a simple request of his guards: "May I be furnished with pen, ink, and paper?"

The request was approved, and André seated himself at a table to compose an honest, forthright, and gentlemanly note to General Washington that confirmed Tallmadge's suspicions and greatest fears. "In this letter," Tallmadge recalled, "he disclosed his Character to be Major John André, Adjutant Genl. to the British Army. When I had perused the letter, which he handed to me to read, my agitation was extreme, and my emotions wholly indescribable."

Though he had no reason to imagine that Arnold would ever turn traitor, Tallmadge had never counted himself among his fans, either. "With Arnold's character I became acquainted while I was a member of Yale College and he residing in New Haven, and I well remember that I was impressed with the belief that he was not a man of integrity," he would later pen. "The revolutionary war was coming on soon after I left college, and Arnold engaged in it with so much zeal . . . we all seemed, as if by common consent, to forget his knavish tricks."

Arnold's backhanded, cowardly character contrasted sharply with that of his coconspirator, André, who comported himself with dignity by all accounts, and treated his captors with respect and even friendliness. Tallmadge could not have helped seeing something of himself reflected back in the person of André. They were both young men—twenty-six and thirty, respectively—entrusted with similar roles of secrecy and responsibility by their countries. Both men had risen to their ranks through hard work, keen intelligence, and personal affability rather than simply through purchasing a commission, as was often the case. They were popular, likable young officers with promising careers ahead of them, and both had gallant manners and a sense of honor that would otherwise seem incongruous with the low opinion of spies in their day.

But this was wartime, and there must be winners

and losers. André had been caught and captured at the same game that Tallmadge was playing; they both knew the rules, the rewards, the risks—and they both knew the penalties.

On October 25, Washington wrote to Jameson regarding the treatment of the high-profile prisoner, noting, "I would not wish Mr. André to be treated with insult; but he . . . is to be most closely and narrowly watched." Then, following his sign-off, Washington added one line as if he were unsure that the seriousness of his message had truly been understood and he wished to underscore this imperative: "André must not escape." Two days later he wrote to Major General Nathanael Greene a similar caution, stating, "I would wish the room for Mr. André to be a decent one, and that he may be treated with civility; but that he may be so guarded as to preclude a possibility of his escaping, which he will certainly attempt to effect, if it shall seem practicable in the most distant degree."

In the tense days that followed, a prisoner exchange was proposed, as was often the case when high-ranking officers were captured. Washington was agreeable only if the prisoner surrendered was Arnold; Clinton would not agree to these terms, so Washington proceeded as he would with any common spy (though, admittedly, perhaps with a little more ceremony given the particular nature of this case). There is every indication that he regretted what came next, but he also knew that it was necessary to demonstrate to the British that his military was to be taken seriously and was operating within its rights as an independent entity not subject to the wishes of the king or his subordinates.

Washington granted André a trial, in which several of the top officers among the Continental Army and its allies were speedily assembled to hear arguments. André maintained that because he had been trapped behind enemy lines and was captured there, he was technically not a spy scouting the territory in the uniform of his service but was, instead, a prisoner of war. All such prisoners, he reasoned, can be expected to at least consider making an escape dressed in civilian clothes. The plea failed to persuade the tribunal, but no one (including André, presumably) had expected it would. He was sentenced to death by hanging on September 29.

That same day, André penned a letter to General Clinton, absolving his commander of any guilt he might feel for the mission on which he had sent André. The circumstances had simply been unfortunate and had not gone according to their carefully laid-out plan:

> *Under these Circumstances I have obtained General Washington's permission to send you this Letter, the object of which is to remove from your Breast any Suspicion that I could imagine that I was bound by your Excellencys Orders to expose myself to what has happened. The Events of coming within an Enemys posts and of Changing my dress which led me to my present Situation were contrary to my own*

Intentions as they were to your Orders; and the circuitous route which I took to return was imposed (perhaps unavoidably) without alternative upon me.

I am perfectly and tranquil in mind and prepared for any Fate to which an honest Zeal for my Kings Service may have devoted me.

In addressing myself to your Excellency on this Occasion, the force of all my Obligations to you and of the Attachment and Gratitude I bear you, recurrs to me. With all the Warmth of my heart I give you thanks for your Excellencys profuse kindness to me, and I send you the most earnest Wishes for your Welfare which a faithfull affectionate and respectfull Attendant can frame.

I have a Mother and Three Sisters. . . . It is needless to be more explicit on this Subject; I am persuaded of your Excellencys Goodness. I receive the greatest Attention from his Excellency General Washington and from every person under whose charge I happened to be placed. I have the honor to be with the most respectfull Attachment,

> *Your Excellencys Most obedient*
> *and most humble Servant,*
> *John André Adj Gen*

The sentence was to be carried out on October 2, just over a week after André's capture. By all accounts, he comported himself with dignity and propriety, stoically recognizing his sad fate as simply one of the unfortunate perils of war. On only one count did he offer up any resistance: manner of execution. André requested to die by firing squad, as the English considered this the proper form by which to carry out execution orders for a high-ranking officer. His request—perhaps in remembrance of Nathan Hale's own unceremonious death—was denied. André was hanged on the appointed day in Tappan, New York, and his body buried under the gallows, where it remained for more than forty years, until it was disinterred and returned to England to be buried with military honors at Westminster Abbey.

BACK IN MANHATTAN

News of Arnold's betrayal, as well as André's capture and execution, sent shock waves through all of the colonies, but nowhere was the impact more keenly felt than in New York City. Even Robert Townsend found himself deeply moved by the death of one of the very men on whom he had spied. "I never felt more sensibly for the death of a person whom I knew only by sight, and had heard converse, than I did for Major André," Townsend wrote to Tallmadge about two weeks after the event. "He was a most amiable character. General Clinton was inconsolable for some days; and the army in general and inhabitants were much exasperated, and think that George Washington must have been destitute of feeling, or he would have saved him. I believe General Washington felt sincerely for him, and would have saved him if it could have been done with propriety." Even Washington himself later reflected that André was "more unfortunate than criminal."

No one had any such praise for Arnold. In his same letter to Tallmadge, Townsend expressed his opinion of the turncoat, probably based on reports of the man's character provided by Agent 355: "I was not much surprised at his [Arnold's] conduct, for it was no more than I expected of him."

Now safely tucked away on a ship in New York, Benedict Arnold was enjoying the luxuries of high living, including the knowledge that his wife and infant son were safe from retribution. He had written to Washington asking if he would guarantee their secure passage to him, and Washington had agreed, not believing it proper to visit the sins of the father upon the head of the child. With Arnold's true loyalties now exposed and his body, mind, and energies openly aligned with the British, he could pose no further threat to American forts or forces under his command.

But Arnold was not finished sowing chaos for the Culper Ring. As Tallmadge had feared, his capture spelled danger for the secret six.

CHAPTER 15

The Ring in Peril

Although Arnold was exposed, the plot to surrender West Point was shattered, and André was dead, the danger to the Culper Ring was still very much alive. "I am happy to think that Arnold does not know my name. However, no person has been taken up on his information," Townsend noted in a letter to Tallmadge. Clearly, Townsend was anticipating what all of the covert operatives must have been dreading—that Arnold would disclose the identities of any spies known to him in order to keep himself in the good graces of the British.

This fear was not paranoia; something similar was certainly happening on the American side, where many of Arnold's comrades and confidants, including the shady Joshua Hett Smith, were being arrested and interrogated to learn who may have been in cahoots with the general and who had merely been manipulated unwittingly. The links of the Culper chain and every independent spy in New York—perhaps in the whole of the colonies—were all on edge, well aware that they would be the target of Arnold's wrath if he had any indication of their identities, and that he was likely to seek revenge on anyone he—or the British— suspected might have had knowledge of any part of the failed plot.

Tallmadge was keenly aware of their concern, and wrote to Washington on October 11:

> *The conduct of Arnold, since his arrival at N.Y. has been such, that though he knows not a single link in the chain of my correspondence, still those who have assisted us in this way, are at present too apprehensive of Danger to give their immediate usual intelligence. I hope as the tumult subsides matters will go on in their old channels.*
>
> *Culper, Junr. has requested an interview with me on Long Island on the 13th inst[ant], but in the present situation of affairs I believe it would be rather imprudent.*

Washington understood the perilous state of all the members of the Culper Ring, and judged Tallmadge's avoidance of a covert visit to Long Island at this particular point in time as quite wise. "I think you were right in declining an interview at this time, as the enemy would act with more than common rigor just now should an officer be taken under circumstances the least suspicious," he wrote back, though he added, "I should be exceedingly glad to hear from C. Junior."

On October 15, Washington wrote to the president of the Continental Congress (at that time, Samuel Huntington of Connecticut), informing him of several matters and noting with regard to Culper Junior: "Unluckily, the person in whom I have the greatest confidence is afraid to take any measures for communicating with me just at this time, as he is apprehensive that Arnold may possibly have some knowledge of the connection, and may have him watched. But as he is assured, that Arnold has not the most distant hint of him, I expect soon to hear from him as usual."

Townsend's return to spying was not as swift as Washington seems to have hoped, however. Woodhull sent a letter dated October 26, in which he explained: "I have this day returned from New York, and am sorry to informe you that the present commotions and watchfullness of the Enemy at New York hath resolved C. Jur. for the present time to quit writing and retire into the country for a time.—Most certainly the enemy are very severe, and the spirits of our friends very low." In an interesting show of steeling his nerves, despite his earlier anxieties—perhaps because he recognized how much safer he was in comparison to the spies who had worked closely with the British officers in New York—Woodhull volunteered his services while Townsend was on hiatus. A few weeks later, he wrote again, "Depend my endeavours shall continue, as I hope never to lose sight of our cause, truly sensible our all is at stake."

A TURN OF AFFAIRS

General Clinton exhibited more humanity than had
Arnold, and promptly released the unfortunate bargemen who had rowed Arnold to the *Vulture*. But that
was the last piece of good news to reach the Americans'
ears for some time. Just as the confusion of the Arnold
betrayal began to dissipate, a blow was struck that
threw all covert agents into a state of fear once again.

Woodhull wrote to Tallmadge, on November 12,
of some disturbing news: "Several of our dear friends
were imprisoned, in particular one that hath been ever
serviceable to this correspondence. This step so dejected the spirits of C. Junr. that he resolved to leave
New York for a time." The letter goes on to add that
Austin Roe had returned from New York and that
Brewster had been pursued and narrowly escaped capture while crossing the Sound. There is no indication
that Rivington was ever suspected or his newspaper
operations suspended, and the ring's satellite members who had functioned as couriers all seemed to be
safe. The person imprisoned was someone who was
known to Townsend and who enjoyed very close ties
to him, making it likely that the "ever serviceable"
friend apprehended was none other than Agent 355.
Whether she was traced by Arnold or caught because
of general suspicion, the lady's capture shattered the
morale of the other five spies.

What could Agent 355 expect to face in a wartime prison? Because no separate women's prison for

combatants existed, Agent 355 would have been held in the primary confinement facility at the time—HMS *Jersey,* anchored in Wallabout Bay, near Brooklyn. Prison ships, often called "death ships" for their deplorable conditions, were routinely used by the British during the war, and the *Jersey* had a reputation for being the worst of the worst, earning the nickname "Hell." Disease and vermin ran rampant among the starving prisoners. The bodies of inmates who died might not be recovered for a week or more, left to rot in the cramped, airless hulls in which the unfortunate passengers were forced to spend twenty-four hours a day. By the end of the war, approximately eight thousand people were estimated to have died aboard prison ships in New York alone.

It is no wonder, then, that Robert Townsend sank into such a deep depression. As Woodhull noted, he temporarily closed his store in Manhattan and returned to Long Island for several weeks to check on the safety of those with whom he had worked, to remove himself (as much as possible) from harm's way, and to try to nurse his spirits back to health even as he mourned the capture and imprisonment of such a brave and faithful friend.

And, as it turns out, the members of the Culper Ring were not the only spies upon whom Arnold had set his sights. A letter to Benjamin Tallmadge on October 25 revealed that Arnold had hopes of persuading the American spymaster himself to follow in his traitorous footsteps:

As I know you to be a man of sense, I am con-
vinced you are by this time fully of opinion that
the real interest and happiness of America con-
sists of a reunion with Great Britain. To effect
which happy purpose I have taken a commission
in the British Army, and invite you to join me
with as many men as you can bring over with
you. If you think proper to embrace my offer, you
shall have the same rank you now hold, in the
Cavalry I am about to raise. I shall make use
of no arguments to convince you, or to induce
you to take a step which I think right. Your own
good sense will suggest everything I can say on the
subject.

Inexplicably, however, the letter did not reach Tallmadge for three months. "I am equally a stranger to the channel through which it was conveyed, the reason why it was so long on its way, or the motives which induced the Traitor to address himself thus particularly to me," Tallmadge wrote to Washington on January 28, 1781. "I have determined to treat the Author with the contempt his conduct merits, by not answering his letter, unless Your Excellency should advise a different Measure."

KIDNAPPING ARNOLD

Even as Townsend was crushed by the news of the capture of fellow agents in the city, on the other side of the matter Arnold found himself somewhat dejected rather quickly as well. Despite his highest hopes and delusions of grandeur, none of his efforts had led to anything particularly fruitful. Even the suspected Patriot spies rounded up in the aftermath of his fleeing to the British failed to yield any more names of coconspirators, which left all of his efforts only half realized and hardly worth the excitement they raised. As a result, he was only paid a total of £6,315 and an annual pension of £360 rather than the full £20,000 on which he had been counting. He was somewhat mollified, however, by receiving a commission in the British army as a brigadier general, which carried with it a fairly respectable salary.

Washington had not given up hope of capturing Arnold. Using the Culper Ring to kidnap the traitor was out of the question—too many of the spies were vulnerable to being known to Arnold, and they were already in enough danger. Instead, Washington commissioned several new spies to make an attempt, explicitly instructing them to bring Arnold back alive to stand trial.

Working covertly with Major Henry Lee—the same Henry Lee who had spoken out against the Intolerable Acts of 1774—Washington devised a daring plan that would require the young officer to operate in complete secrecy and to disavow any involvement on the general's part. A sergeant named John Champe volunteered to carry out a dangerous mission, the particular details of which he learned only after stepping forward. "[Champe] was about twenty three or twenty four years of age," Lee later recalled in his *Memoirs of the War in the Southern Department of the United States,* and "rather above the common size, full of bone and muscle, with a saturnine countenance, grave thoughtful and taciturne, of tried courage and inflexible perseverance." In short, he was large, strong, serious, and stubborn—the perfect man for such a difficult job.

His mission was to desert from Lee's Second Partisan Corps and join the British in New York City as a defector. If he implied that he had been inspired by Arnold's actions, he stood a chance of meeting Arnold and gaining his confidence. Once ingratiated with Arnold, he was to study his routines and habits and discover the most efficient means of kidnapping him with the help of a handful of operatives in and around Manhattan. The men would then smuggle the traitor out of the city and back into American-held territory in New Jersey, where Washington could take custody of Arnold.

Champe and his associates needed to be extremely careful, however, for Washington did not want to give the British any reason to believe that the Americans had simply sent in thugs to finish off Arnold as revenge. The general wrote to Lee on October 20: "No circumstance whatever shall obtain my consent to his being put to death. The idea which would accompany such an event would be that Ruffians had been hired to assassinate him. My aim is to make a public example of him, and this should be strongly impressed upon those who are employed to bring him off."

The plan worked beautifully. Champe managed to successfully desert, though the extreme secrecy of the plan meant that Lee's unsuspecting men gave chase and nearly captured Champe to bring him back for punishment. Nevertheless, he made it to the shore not far from two British ships and dove into the water, swimming madly toward them. After he was taken aboard and questioned, the British brought him into the city, where General Clinton, upon interviewing him, deemed his desire to join the British genuine, introduced him to Arnold, and placed him in the force Arnold now commanded.

Over the next few weeks he formed a plan to capture Arnold during his evening walk. However, Champe never turned up on the evening of December 21, when he was scheduled to bring an unconscious Arnold to a small boat waiting in the river. A few days later, it was learned that Arnold's unit (in which Champe was now serving as part of his cover) had been unexpectedly shipped off to Virginia the day before. What had begun as a promising attempt to purchase additional safety for the Culpers by removing a dangerous enemy ended in disappointment.

SMALL VICTORIES

Despite the clever plotting of Washington and Lee and the valiant efforts of John Champe, Benedict Arnold was still at large, which meant the Culper Ring was still at risk—and one of them was still imprisoned. The pressure was felt by every member, but the spy at the center of the ring suffered the most.

Evidence of Townsend's continued anxiety and despondency throughout the fall and winter of 1780–81 shows up in the account book from his store. Whereas he had previously been quite prompt in recording his business transactions, the entries suddenly appear far more sporadic. Between November 1779 and July 1780, he updated his accounts every three to five days at first, then slowed down to every seven to nine days. During those eight months, he was almost predictable in his reckonings, with the exception of February–March 1780, when he twice lapsed thirteen days between entries. During the summer of 1780, his entries began to have much larger spans between them. He made no entries for September, just one in October (on the seventh), and then nothing again until December 2. The next time he seems to have cracked open his ledger after that was nearly four months later, on March 29, 1781.

Townsend's spying activities largely ceased during the season of his withdrawal from business, but Washington took advantage of that time to shift his focus temporarily from Manhattan to the surrounding areas. Thanks in part to the reports still coming in from Woodhull on Long Island, Washington began to reconsider Tallmadge's earlier proposals to storm certain vulnerable locations on the island.

On November 21, 1780, Tallmadge (now a colonel in the Continental Army) led a contingency of eighty men selected from his Second Dragoons—along with Caleb Brewster, who is listed as a captain in the operation—from Fairfield, Connecticut, across Long Island Sound in whaleboats to the town of Mount Sinai, roughly six miles from Tallmadge's native Setauket. Battling rain and high winds, they marched roughly twenty miles through the night of the twenty-second, straight across the island to Mastic, on the southern shore, and attacked Fort St. George on the morning of November 23. Constructed and fortified the previous year by staunch Loyalists and named for the patron saint of England, the fort had a large stockpile of supplies and provisions, including an ample supply of hay upon which British soldiers in the area depended to feed their livestock. After a brief fight against the well-armed residents, Tallmadge's men were able to seize control, destroy the stockpile, burn the hay, and take the fort's inhabitants prisoner—all with suffering only one injury on their side. The prisoners were marched back across the island to the boats that were waiting under guard, and the whole company crossed the Sound again for Connecticut.

Washington was pleased by the efforts and applauded Tallmadge in a personal letter. Woodhull, too, sent his congratulations, writing on November 28, "The burning the forage is agreeable to me and must hurt the enemy much."

It was not a major battle from a strategic standpoint, but it delivered an important morale boost to the Patriots and provided a psychological victory over the British by proving that New York and Long Island had not been forgotten, nor were they invincible.

CHAPTER 16

The Beginning of the End

With the death of André, the British found themselves without a spymaster at a time when such an officer was particularly important. Things were heating up in the south again, particularly in Virginia, where Arnold (with poor Champe in tow) had sailed with fifteen hundred troops in December 1780. Clinton found his attentions drawn to the Chesapeake even as the raid at Fort St. George had proved that New York could not be left unattended. A man was named to fill André's vacancy and manage intelligence for the commander of the British troops on American soil.

Major Oliver DeLancey was in his early thirties—a New York City native whose family was among the earliest Jewish settlers in the American colonies. He had been educated in England but returned home soon after the war began in order to organize a Loyalist regiment in New York. He may not have had the same level of star appeal that André enjoyed, but he was brilliant, able, and now operating in his native territory, which gave him a distinct advantage in understanding the people, customs, and terrain. He immediately set about to reorganize the British intelligence system, unifying codes and bringing a number of disparate and independent elements together so that information could more easily be shared, analyzed, and acted upon.

The Culper Ring, in the meantime, stayed busy (if not active in spying) as the calendar turned from 1780 to 1781. Late in the winter, Caleb Brewster captured a British boat and eight prisoners, including two officers. Townsend resumed his business and reopened his shop in the city in March. Woodhull tried to persuade him to start gathering intelligence again, but Townsend believed that the British had dispatched a spy of their own in New York who was actively trying to root out the sources and paths of the Culpers' information and insisted on lying low. The matter was dropped until the end of April, when Tallmadge could finally report the pending resurrection of the ring's activities, with a few adjustments made to their former routine. "The plan which he [Woodhull] has consented to adopt, on certain conditions, is for him to remain for the most part on Long Island and C. Junr. whom he thinks might be engaged again, to reside constantly at New York," he wrote to Washington on the twenty-fifth. "That some confidential person must of course be employed to carry dispatches as it would cause suspicions which might lead to detection if either of the Culpers should be frequently passing from

New York to Setauket, &c. they being men of some considerable note."

Washington preferred a more timely delivery of intelligence, but he agreed to this arrangement. The Culpers' reports were essential to the continued success of the Americans, even if they did take a few days longer to arrive. The general had learned from his earlier mistake; vital information received a few days late was infinitely preferable to no information at all. He quickly replied to Tallmadge:

> *The great object of information you are very well acquainted with—such as, Arrivals, Embarkations, Preparations for Movements, alterations of Positions, situation of Posts, Fortifications, Garrisons, strength or weakness of each, distributions and strength of Corps, and in general every thing which can be interesting and important for us to know. Besides these, upon a smaller scale, which are necessary to be reported: and that whatever intelligence is communicated ought to be not in general terms, but in detail, and with the greatest precision.*
>
> *At present I am anxious to know (for the reports have been very numerous vague and uncertain) whether another embarkation is preparing, and if so to what amount, and where destined. What the present force of the Enemy is; particularly on Long Island, in New York and at King's Bridge. What Corps are at the latter place, how strong, and where*

posted exactly—and indeed what the situation, prospect, and designs of the enemy are, so far as they can be penetrated into.

Washington's instructions are vast in their scope and display the extreme confidence he had in his most valuable ring to obtain precisely the breadth and depth of intelligence he required. He took pains in the same letter to note that he was "engaging in behalf of the United States a liberal reward for the services of the C——s, (of whose fidelity and ability I entertain a high opinion) it is certainly but reasonable, from patriotism and every other principle, that their exertions should be proportionally great, to subserve essentially the interest of the Public."

Despite Washington's praise, Townsend adamantly refused to put pen to paper. He had seen how André had been done in by the discovery of papers and plans— hard and damning evidence he could not deny or talk his way out of. He would be happy to convey orally whatever information he had observed, Townsend explained to Woodhull when they met in the city in early May, but the risk of trying to smuggle written documents out of Manhattan was far too great. Woodhull could not deny the truth of those concerns, especially now that Oliver DeLancey was asserting his authority with new ideas for uncovering plots in their midst.

In his May 19 letter to Tallmadge, Woodhull noted that, on the way back to Long Island from visiting Townsend, "the enemy must have got some hint of me for when passing at Brooklyn Ferry was strictly exam-

ined and told some vilian supported a correspondence
from this place." The letter also included intelligence
Austin Roe had obtained verbally from Townsend
on his last visit to the city, but they all knew their
visits could not be so frequent as to raise suspicions.
Woodhull and Townsend worked exhaustively to recruit a new member for the ring, one who was not already under the watchful eyes of British operatives
and could operate freely in Manhattan and smuggle
out detailed written reports. "When at New York myself, together with Culper Junior [we] almost racked
our invention to point out a proper person and made
several attempts but failed—no person will write,"
Woodhull lamented.

SECRET SIX DELIVER YORKTOWN TO
WASHINGTON

General Washington remained hopeful that the next
major military engagement would be focused on retak-
ing New York, but he was depending heavily on the
French navy—specifically, the large fleet under the command of Admiral François-Joseph-Paul de Grasse,
which was currently in the Caribbean—because the
success of the mission would rely in large part upon
the men, supplies, and ships that the French could provide to shore up the inadequately manned and provi-
sioned American forces. This meant that Washington's
plans were at the mercy of the French leaders who ordered the admiral to sail. So when word reached the
general that the fleet would be sailing in August 1781 to

Yorktown, Virginia, and not to New York, he was disappointed but knew he could not afford to squander such an opportunity—especially because he had a secret weapon.

By leaving a small contingency of twenty-five hundred men north of New York and ordering another unit to fake preparations for storming Staten Island, Washington gambled that the feints would frustrate General Clinton and leave him unsure of whether or not he could afford to send reinforcements to help out Lieutenant General Charles Cornwallis, one of Britain's most esteemed and feared generals, at Yorktown. Meanwhile, Washington led his troops on a miserable, sweaty summer march southward to the malarial swamps of eastern Virginia.

At roughly the same time, Allen McLane—the same McLane who had harbored suspicions against Benedict Arnold in Philadelphia in 1778—had been ordered to Long Island to gather any information he could regarding the preparations of the British ships set to bring relief and, presumably, to meet with the agents already working there who could provide him with a fuller picture before he slipped back out to rejoin Washington's troops as they made camp at Yorktown. McLane had special instructions to learn as many of the British navy's code signals as possible, so that the French fleet could decipher what the enemy ships were communicating to one another during naval engagements. It was a nearly impossible task, because ships in harbor are unlikely to use distress codes or signals for attack, so McLane was left to try any desperate or accidental manner he could devise to piece together the secret system—an ineffective (not to mention dangerous) approach.

Fortunately, while on Long Island, McLane was put into contact with James Rivington. The printer and coffeehouse owner was still operating his presses and still fraternizing with the British in Manhattan despite the dangers to spies, and his persistence had paid off. Whether someone had left a copy in Rivington's coffeehouse or the British had commissioned him to print additional copies is not clear, but somehow he managed to procure a copy of the entire British naval codebook. Rivington passed it on to McLane, who rushed it to Washington.

Both McLane and the codebook made it safely off Long Island and down to Virginia by the end of the summer, and Washington was able to transport the book to Admiral de Grasse's custody by mid-September. In French hands, it was a more effective resource than the Americans could have dared hope for, and its loss was more devastating than the British could have imagined.

The siege of Yorktown was a roaring success, thanks in no small part to de Grasse's ability to anticipate nearly every movement of the British fleet. Paralyzed by indecision for fear of leaving New York vulnerable to attack, and despite continued assurances to Cornwallis that he would send reinforcements, General Clinton failed to deliver any of the promised troops to Virginia. Trapped by both land and sea, Cornwallis was unable to muster the power to break through in either direction. He could not attack; he could not retreat. A white flag was the only option. He surrendered on October 19.

The defeat at Yorktown was an embarrassment to the entire British military and caused a tremendous spat between Clinton and Cornwallis that became a public scandal back in Britain. Cornwallis set sail on the same ship that carried Benedict Arnold and his family to London in January 1782; once on English soil he was able to perform some measure of damage control by speaking critically of Clinton's leadership. Clinton submitted his resignation as the commander in chief for North America and departed for England in mid-May. In 1783, he published a book narrating his account of the 1781 campaign in North America, in which he wrote that Cornwallis's failings ultimately led to the defeat at Yorktown.

To military leaders on both sides, however, the events at Yorktown made it clear that the conflict was reaching its natural end. The Americans had stood their ground and doggedly fought for every inch of land they deemed rightfully their own; the British government was finally recognizing that superior military muscle was not enough to make the determined Patriot army back down when they had powerful allies on their side. On March 28, 1782, word reached New York from London that the House of Commons had voted to end all offensive strikes in the American colonies, though that by no means signified the end of military occupation or exercises. At the same time, a more moderate prime minister was coming to power backed by a Parliament that generally opposed the war. An end to the hostilities seemed inevitable, but matters were far from settled.

Savannah, Charleston, and New York still remained strongholds of the British army, and Washington was forced to decide, in the critical weeks following Yorktown, if he should continue to march southward and eliminate those threats before refocusing his energies and resources northward on New York. In the end, he decided to divide his forces, sending some to strengthen the beleaguered troops in the Carolinas and Georgia but returning with the majority of his troops to the Hudson Valley, just above the city. He was sure that the British were not going to allow New York to fall without a fight.

CHANGING TIDES IN NEW YORK

Unrest was erupting throughout the city. The pockets of Patriot dissidents who had dug in their heels and stayed during the long duration of the war now grew bolder while Loyalists who had been certain of coming out of the war on the winning side felt betrayed by the Crown. Broadsides and other printed matter began to appear posted on walls and clutched in citizens' hands. New Yorkers vented discontentment with various politicians, with the king, with the war in general. Rumors of peace negotiations between the two delegations began to trickle in via packet ships, and all wondered what the terms of peace might be. Sir Guy Carleton assumed the role of commander in chief from Clinton in May 1782, which only added to the feelings of uncertainty, transition, and unrest even as the British government seemed to turn away from all interest in a continued investment in the American conflict.

The British officers garrisoned in New York feared an uprising from within by emboldened Patriots almost as much as they feared an external attack from the Continental Army. Both out of desperation and as a show of power, the British military began enacting impressment measures around the city, pulling civilians out of their ordinary lives to serve in temporary guard duties for king and country, as Carleton's tight command of the city made Clinton's authority seem paltry. Woodhull remarked on this trend when he wrote to Tallmadge on July 5:

> *Their design appears only to act on the defensive and be as little expense to the Crown as possible. God grant their time may be short for we have much reason to fear within their lines that Carlton's finger will be heavier than Clinton's Thigh. Carlton's called a Tyrant at New York by the inhabitants in general and makes them do Soldiers duty in the city without distinction. The first Gentlemen in the City stand at Officer's doors Soldier like.*

Robert Townsend may have been one of these unwilling temporary recruits. Family tradition held that years later a British uniform was found stored with his belongings; when questioned about it, he reluctantly spoke of having been impressed into standing watch at the officers' headquarters in New York.

In July 1782, the British left Savannah. There was no doubt that the war would soon be officially over, with the Americans emerging victorious; all but the most ardent and desperate Tories recognized that only the formal terms of a peace treaty needed to be established before the remaining enemy troops would be forced to leave the soil of the sovereign, independent United States of America.

Loyalists now had a difficult choice to make: Did they stay and rebuild their lives, or did they emigrate back to Europe or northward to Canada? There was some hope, at first, that any lands and property formerly in Tory hands would be returned if they had been seized during the war; however, most people recognized that such a measure would be difficult to carry out and, in some cases, might actually pose a threat to the new nation, especially if large tracts of acreage ended up back in the hands of those who remained loyal to the king and wished to revive hostilities. Besides, the reasoning was "To the victors go the spoils"—even if that seemed unfortunate and unjust. The majority of Loyalists, like the majority of Patriots (and the revolutionary agnostics), were humble men and women of modest means: small landowners, tenant farmers, laborers in the cities, fishermen and longshoremen along the coasts, hunters and traders in the frontiers of the Appalachians. Any property they possessed likely had not been, nor would be, threatened by seizure. In deciding where to live out the remainder of their days, they had to take into consideration the inclinations of their neighbors and their own consciences; it would not be a pleasant thing to be forever regarded as "the neighbor who fought against our government." Some of the wealthiest citizens had already booked passage back to England; now the common folk began to do the same.

Each packet ship that arrived in New York Harbor carried more news from England and less hope that King George would prevail, or that those subjects who had professed fidelity to him would receive any kind of reward for their loyalty and faith in the most powerful military on earth.

TOWNSEND'S LAST LETTER

As Robert Townsend rode into Westchester County, New York, he could not have helped but admire the beauty of the foliage and the crispness in the September air. Nearly six years to the day after Nathan Hale's hanging, here was another spy carrying his reports on New York directly to Benjamin Tallmadge, and from Tallmadge's hand they would reach Washington.

It was an unlikely meeting in several ways. Not long ago, the ride west from New York City to Westchester would have been barred by sentries and checkpoints. It was still heavily guarded, that was true—the British did not want to let go of New York until absolutely required to do so, and they knew Washington was prowling outside, ready to pounce at his first opportunity—but one could now pass more safely into

American-held territory without having to traverse the same tricky no-man's-land that had ensnared André.

It was also an unlikely meeting because Townsend had firmly declined to commit anything to writing back in May. But now he could see the shaky position of the city and knew that Washington needed the best intelligence he could offer in order to calculate the next—and maybe final—move of the war. Townsend shouldered the responsibility of delivering the latest report himself, figuring that at this late point in the war with all that had already transpired, if he was arrested and tried as a spy he would have only himself to blame.

Finally, the meeting was unlikely because Townsend was carrying news that the war was nearly over. Despite the British hold on New York, the Americans were in position to secure their independence, thanks in no small part to the Culper Ring.

The message Townsend delivered to Tallmadge, with the date September 19, 1782, written across the top, is the final surviving letter from Culper Junior's hand. The news painted a city in upheaval:

> *The last packet [ship], so far from bringing better news to the loyalists, has indeed brought the clearest and unequivocal Proofs that the independence of America is unconditionally to be acknowledged, nor will there be any conditions insisted on for those who joined the King's Standard.*
>
> *It is said that an Expedition is now forming at N.Y. and by many conjectured to be against*

the French Fleet &c. at Boston; a number of British Troops were embarking when I left the city on the 14th and 15th inst[ant]. But I conversed fully with one of Carleton's Aides on this subject, who told me that I might depend they were bound to the W. Indies or Halifax. For my own part I have no expectation that they think of any offensive movements. The above gentleman, with whom I am most intimately connected, informed me that it is now under consideration to send all the B. Troops to the West Indies.

. . . It is a fact that a fleet is going to Charlestown to bring off that Garrison.

. . . Sir Guy himself says that he thinks it not improbable that the next Packet may bring orders for an evacuation of N. York.

A fleet is getting ready to sail for the Bay of Fundy about the first of October to transport a large number of Refugees to that Quarter. The Aide above referred to informs us that he thinks it probable he shall go there himself. Indeed, I never saw such general distress and dissatisfaction in my life as is painted in the countenance of every Tory at N.Y.

The Beef Contractors had orders a few days past to cease purchasing any more for the Navy and from the appearance of things the whole fleet are getting ready for a movement.

I am myself uncertain when the Troops will leave N.Y. but I must confess I rather

believe if the King's Magazines can be removed,
that they will leave us this fall.

Unfortunately for Washington, Townsend's prediction of a British evacuation before the end of 1782 proved a little too optimistic. In Paris, where John Adams, Benjamin Franklin, John Jay, and Henry Laurens were representing the American government, negotiations were dragging on with no sign of resolution. Even after Charleston was abandoned to the Americans on December 14 and South Carolina could boast its freedom from the Crown, Sir Guy Carleton stayed planted firmly and stubbornly in New York with no plans to move until ordered to do so by King George himself. The toll on life and property that would result from an attack on New York no longer seemed worth the risk to Washington, but he could not celebrate victory (nor could any of the citizens) until a binding treaty had been ratified and New York—and America—had rid itself of foreign occupation.

CHAPTER 17

Retaking New York at Last

The year 1783 dawned full of promise. On February 3, the government of Great Britain formally acknowledged the independence of what were once its American colonies as the United States of America. The following day it agreed to halt all military involvement. In April, a preliminary peace treaty was ratified, and in July tracts of land in Canada were opened to Loyalists seeking a new life and a region was designated for former slaves who had fought for Britain. Crowded ships bound for Nova Scotia and New Brunswick sailed northward from New York Harbor. But still, the British army remained firmly and fixedly in Manhattan.

North of the city, near his encampment in Newburgh, Washington was struggling to subdue a rising insurrection against the back wages owed and promises of land that had been offered to Patriot soldiers but which Congress had failed so far to deliver. Combat may have reached an end, but the enemy still would not leave and the daunting task of rebuilding the country while paying down the debts of war loomed as challenges still to be faced.

Woodhull, meanwhile, continued to send the occasional report from Long Island, though there was nothing of great urgency or importance anymore. The Culpers had done their duty, and done it well. A note dated July 5, 1783, was accompanied by a final balance record that Woodhull submitted to Tallmadge, at the major's request: "I only kept the most simple account that I possibly could, for fear it should betray me, but I trust it is a just one—and I do assure you I have been as frugal as possibly could. I desire you would explain to the Genl. the circumstances that attended this lengthy correspondence that he may be satisfied that we have not been extravagant." Woodhull then concluded the letter in a way that clearly reflected the present optimistic mood on Long Island: "Wishing you health and happiness, I am your very humble servant, Sam¹. Culper."

After five years, four major plots thwarted, countless misgivings and close calls, and untold sleepless nights, the Culper correspondence came to an end. The ring had operated effectively from the very heart of the enemy's headquarters and had never been successfully infiltrated, uncovered, or unmasked, despite numerous efforts in that vein. The loss of Agent 355 was a tragedy, but it was also remarkable that the casualties were not much higher given how close the Culpers were to the enemy in Manhattan and the daring movements and maneuvers of the agents on Long

Island. While the spies had not been able to deliver
Manhattan to Washington before the war's end, they
had been his eyes and ears there, enabling him to beat
the British even without holding the city. The Culper
Ring was a success.

All that remained now between Washington and
his spies was the settling of some small monetary
debts; the larger debts—the intangible kind that
helped to protect a fledgling nation—could never be
fully repaid, nor did the remaining members of the
Culper Ring seek out such payment. A return to an
open, honest, and simple life in an independent nation
founded on their native soil would be reward enough.
And so they hoped, and prayed, and waited for the
British to depart from New York at long last, even as
the aftermath of war swirled around them.

PEACE RAGES

The British delegation finally signed the Treaty of Paris
in September, and Washington's troops were at the
ready to ride into Manhattan as the last redcoat left the
city. Colonel Tallmadge, however, was concerned for
the safety of his spies who had lived and worked as Loyalists during the occupation and might now find themselves threatened by their newly empowered Patriot
neighbors who had no inkling of their true sentiments
and bravery. How could Townsend erase the fact that
he had run a store that served British soldiers, worked
for a Loyalist newspaper, frequented the coffeehouse
popular among the officers, and kept company with

those who had penetrated the inner circles of the top brass in the city?

To anyone on the outside, Robert Townsend had not only enjoyed a rather cushy life during the war but also profited from it. This would hardly sit well with those who had suffered the loss of life, limb, and property for the sake of American independence, and Colonel Tallmadge was fearful that some vengeful Patriot might come looking for his pound of flesh. He was desperate to seek out his spies and contract bodyguards to ensure their personal welfare, send them underground, create for them yet another false identity elsewhere in the city, or even spirit them out of New York for a time until passions cooled.

Tallmadge wrote in his memoirs of these concerns:

> As little doubt could be entertained but that peace would soon follow, I found it necessary to take some steps to insure the safety of several persons within the enemy's lines, who had served us faithfully and with intelligence during the war. As some of these were considered to be of the Tory character . . . I suggested to Gen. Washington the propriety of my being permitted to go to New York, under the cover of a flag. This he very readily granted, and I proceeded to New York, where I was surrounded by British troops, tories, cowboys, and traitors.

The whole experience of crossing into Manhattan must have been rather surreal for Tallmadge, as he enjoyed the unusual privilege of dining with General Carleton himself, and noted that "by the officers of the army and navy I was treated with great respect and attention." He added, "It was not a little amusing to see how men, tories and refugees, who a little before uttered nothing but the terms, *rebels and traitors to their King*, against all the officers of the American army, would now come around me while in New York, and beg my protection against the dreaded rage of their countrymen."

Despite the various distractions, the bids for his attention, and his high-profile status, Tallmadge was able to meet quietly and safely with Townsend and the others he was seeking out to ensure their security when the British finally evacuated the city. "While at New York I saw and secured all who had been friendly to us through the war, and especially our emissaries," he wrote. Then he rode north again to Newburgh to wait for Washington's next orders:

> *Having accomplished all my business in New York, I returned again to the army, and made my report to the Commander-in-Chief. The troops now began to be impatient to return to their respective homes, and those that were destined for that purpose, to take possession of the city. Gen. Washington now dismissed the greater part of the army in so judicious a way, that no unpleasant circumstances occurred.*

The troops broke camp and returned home, their service completed and their dreams for liberty real-

ized. Only those soldiers appointed to ride into New
York with Washington stayed on, eager and grateful to
be part of that historic moment.

FINALLY BACK IN NEW YORK

At noon on Tuesday, November 25, 1783—coincidentally,
the same date as Robert Townsend's thirtieth birthday—
Washington rode into Manhattan, with Benjamin Tallmadge among the officers at his side. A contingent rode
ahead, scanning the streets as the last of the British officers boarded their ships; Washington followed with
his officers and troops spanning eight across. In the
previous days and hours leading up to that moment,
some joyful Patriots had hoisted American flags over
their homes only to have them torn down; in a few
cases, they came to blows with the redcoat enforcers.
But now the citizens of New York, no longer subject to
British law or British soldiers, waved flags freely as
Washington rode forward. Church bells tolled not in
warning but in celebration, and the shouts after each
firing of the cannons were triumphant rather than terrified. Some people even crowded at the water's edge,
waving at the ships set for departure and laughingly
bidding the defeated soldiers on board a lovely trip
home. "So perfect was the order of march, that entire
tranquility prevailed, and nothing occurred to mar the
general joy," Tallmadge wrote.

*Every countenance seemed to express the tri-
umph of republican principles over the military*

despotism which had so long pervaded this now
happy city. Most of the refugees had embarked for
Nova Scotia, and the few who remained, were too
insignificant to be noticed in the crowd. It was
indeed a joyful day to the officers and soldiers of
our army, and to all the friends of American in-
dependence, while the troops of the enemy, still in
our waters, and the host of tories and refugees,
were sorely mortified. The joy of meeting friends,
who had long been separated by the cruel rigors
of war, cannot be described.

The next nine days were filled with celebrations and
visitations as Washington toured the city. As his step-
grandson, George Washington Parke Custis, would
later record, the general even made a special stop at the
shop of James Rivington, much to the surprise of many
of the officers in his company, who considered Rivington a Loyalist scoundrel whose continued presence in
the newly freed New York seemed an affront to all Patriots. But Washington seemed purposeful, even determined, as he excused himself to speak privately with
Rivington about (so he claimed) certain books that the
printer intended to order from London. The two men
disappeared briefly, then came back to the front room,
where Washington prepared to take his leave.

"Your Excellency may rely upon my especial attention being given to the agricultural works," Rivington
said as he escorted the party to the door, voicing the
sentiments most dear to the tired general's heart at that
moment, "which, on their arrival, will be immediately

forwarded to Mount Vernon, where I trust they will contribute to your gratification amid the shades of domestic retirement."

At noon on December 4, Washington met with his officers in Fraunces Tavern, just a few blocks from Rivington's establishment and the Fly Market, where Robert Townsend had operated his shop and carried out his spying duties. "The time now drew near when the Commander-in-Chief intended to leave this part of the country for his beloved retreat at Mount Vernon," Tallmadge recorded in his memoirs, adding that "it was made known to the officers then in New York, that Gen. Washington intended to commence his journey on that day."

Entering the room promptly at twelve o'clock, Washington seated himself and enjoyed a light lunch before raising his glass of wine; speaking in a voice heavy with emotion, he told them: "With a heart full of love and gratitude I now take leave of you. I most devoutly wish that your latter days may be as prosperous and happy as your former ones have been glorious and honorable."

Following the toast, Washington paused before adding, "[I] shall feel obliged if each of you will come and take me by the hand." One by one, the officers silently came forward to embrace the general.

"The *simple thought* that we were then about to part from the man who had conducted us through a long and bloody war . . . and that we should see his face no more in this world, seemed to me utterly insupportable," Tallmadge wrote. A solemn procession marched Washington to the docks, where he would begin his journey home to Virginia. He was a tired man who earnestly believed his life of public service was over, and that the next generation would be those called upon to lead the country through the coming years. Tallmadge narrated the scene with a note of finality:

> *We all followed in mournful silence to the wharf, where a prodigious crowd had assembled to witness the departure of the man who, under God, had been the great agent in establishing the glory and independence of these United States. As soon as he was seated, the barge put off into the river, and when out in the stream, our great and beloved General waived his hat, and bid us a silent adieu.*

"WE THE PEOPLE"

Not long after General Washington's departure for civilian life, his brothers in arms followed suit. "In a few days," Tallmadge recorded, "all the officers who had assembled at New York to participate in the foregoing heart-rending scene, departed to their several places of abode, to commence anew their avocations for life." They could, at long last, enjoy the future for which they had all so gallantly fought.

Tallmadge, too, returned home to a memorable celebration he described in rather poetic terms in his memoirs:

> *Having for seven years been banished from the home of my father, at Brookhaven, in Suffolk*

county, on Long Island, I determined to visit the place of my nativity. . . . Being principally Whigs, and now emancipated from their late severe bondage, the people had determined that they would celebrate the occasion by some public demonstration of their joy. They therefore concluded to have public notice given, that on a day near at hand, they would have an ox roasted whole on the public green, to partake of which all were invited to attend. I remember well, that after a most joyful meeting with my former friends (many of whom I had not seen since the war commenced), I was appointed master of ceremonies for the occasion. When the ox was well roasted, the noble animal on his spit was removed to a proper place, and after a blessing from the God of Battles had been invoked by my honored father, I began to carve, dissect, and distribute to the multitude around me. The aged and the young, the male and the female, rejoiced to receive a portion, which, from the novelty of the scene, and being in commemoration of so great an event, obtained a particular zest. All was harmony and joy, for all seemed to be of one mind.

A Tory could not have lived in that atmosphere one minute. . . . The joy of the Whig population through the island was literally unbounded.

Tallmadge then set out to ride eastward across Long Island to visit friends and survey the land. As he rode from town to town, he was quite delighted to find that the Patriotic fervor had not been lost by those citizens who had endured much suffering under the rule of the British and the political dominance of the Loyalists: "Private hospitality and public honor were most liberally bestowed on any man who had served in the revolutionary army."

As picturesque as Tallmadge's transition back to civilian life was, his former commander George Washington would not have long to enjoy his own "shades of domestic retirement," as James Rivington had wished for him. Despite making every effort to remain out of the public eye, on April 30, 1789, Washington once again found himself in New York City, the capital of the new nation. This time, however, his hand was resting not upon his sword but upon a Bible as he was sworn in to the office of president of the United States. He had not wanted the position and had only accepted reluctantly when he was finally persuaded that his leadership would help unify the former colonies of the infant nation that were still struggling on wobbling legs toward complete self-governance free of foreign presence or occupation. Washington also declined all other titles and honoraria other than the simple and direct address of "Mr. President."

A DISAPPOINTING VISIT

The following year, Washington made a tour of Long Island to meet the people and examine the damage done to land and property during the British occupation. But he also had it in mind to privately visit with and thank the individuals who had risked so much to gather intelligence and smuggle it to him.

He approached Setauket on April 22, 1790, and made a stop at "the House of a Capt. Roe, which is tolerably dect. with obliging people in it." Whether those obliging people with whom he passed several pleasant hours included the rest of the Setauket Culpers—Benjamin Tallmadge, Abraham Woodhull, and Caleb Brewster—or if he was even aware that he was lodging under the roof of one of those very spies he had journeyed to thank, Washington did not say. His knowledge of the ring members' true identities was, after all, quite limited by design. He had not wanted to know more than he needed to in order to protect them, and several of the members (Townsend in particular) had been insistent that Washington never learn their names. The following day he took his leave of Roe's tavern and continued westward, where his tour took him to Oyster Bay. His brief notes make no mention of a meeting with Robert Townsend or any member of his family, despite the senior Samuel's numerous run-ins with the law and his suffering as Colonel Simcoe's reluctant landlord. Had Washington been aware of the debt of gratitude that he owed to a certain native son of this town, his stay surely would not have been so brief. Instead, he made his visit, paid his respects to the brave citizens of the town, and rode on, having never met the man he so earnestly sought to thank.

By the time the president crossed the ferry back to

Manhattan at sundown on April 24, he had completed his circuit around the part of the island wherein lived the ring of spies who had served him so faithfully and carried out their weighty task with such dedication and courage. He had sincerely hoped to have some time with the mysterious Culper Junior, who had risked his life, health, and well-being for so long, passing in and out of the lion's mouth every day, seeking to still the monarch's roar within American borders. But no matter the greetings sent the general's way and the invitations extended, Townsend never stepped out of the shadows to meet with his commander in chief. It was a great honor, to be sure, but not one that Townsend sought. He did not want praise or celebration; the greatest reward Washington could give him was simply a return to a quiet and unassuming life as a man subject to no king but God.

Those few who knew the Culpers' secret kept it close, and all Washington could do was carry in his heart the gratitude he had for the sacrifices of his brave spies, which were no less meaningful for having been made in city streets and country back roads as on a battlefield. For these men and women, too, had given their all to "establish Justice, insure domestic Tranquility, provide for the common defence, promote the general Welfare, and secure the Blessings of Liberty to ourselves and our Posterity."

CHAPTER 18

Life After the Ring

With the end of the war and the start of the American republic, the Culpers could return to their lives as ordinary citizens. While a few were not shy about their role in the war effort and enjoyed a bit of notoriety for their daring adventures, most did what all good spies do: They carried on in obscurity as ordinary and unassuming people whose neighbors never knew they had led double lives. Their stories were packed away like pressed flowers in the pages of a book—quietly waiting, undetected for years—to reward some curious reader decades later with the intricacy and beauty of their design. There were whispers, rumors, and legends, of course—but no one pursued them, happy to leave well enough alone when the desired outcome of liberty had been reached, though at a high and terrible cost.

Caleb Brewster, after his years of excitement rowing back and forth across Long Island Sound in his whaleboat and engaging in hard-fought skirmishes, found that the second part of his life was much quieter than the first, though he was never far from the sea. He married Anne Lewis of Fairfield, Connecticut, in 1784, and moved to a farm at Black Rock, southwest of Bridgeport, where the couple had several children. Brewster passed away at his farm on February 13, 1827, and for all of his prodigious feats of bravery and skill during the war, his headstone notes his eventual rank of captain and then sums up his service simply: "He was a brave and active officer of the Revolution."

James Rivington had a less tranquil retirement. According to George Washington Parke Custis, during the private meeting between Washington and Rivington in the bookshop, the officers in the front room could distinctly hear a bag of gold coins being handed to the bookseller for his spying services during the war. Custis, however, was not actually present for the events and had a habit of occasionally embellishing stories in accordance with his own imagination. Whether gold really changed hands during this meeting or not remains unclear. But what is certain is that Rivington and his shop received special protection in the days and weeks following the British evacuation; there would be no burning and looting as had occurred at the hands of the Sons of Liberty in 1775. Later correspondence of Washington's confidants defended Rivington against libel. He remained in New York, though his newspaper business suffered because of his reputation as a staunch enemy of the new republic. He was eventually forced to close his shop, but with eight children to support back in England, several bad investments, and a personal taste for the high life, his financial situation deteriorated until he was forced to serve time in debtors' prison. He died in New York, where he had spent thirty-six of his seventy-eight years of life, on July 4, 1802.

Austin Roe, like Caleb Brewster, achieved the rank of captain and carried that title proudly for the rest of his life. He and his wife, the former Catherine Jones, had eight children; in 1798, the family moved from Setauket, on the north shore of Long Island, to Patchogue, almost exactly opposite on the southern shore, and opened a hotel. Unlike many of the other Culpers, Roe enjoyed sharing stories of his spying adventures with locals and patrons at his inn, though he was careful to protect the privacy of his fellow ring members. He passed away on November 29, 1830, at the age of eighty-one.

Benjamin Tallmadge married Mary Floyd, daughter of Major General William Floyd, a signer of the Declaration of Independence. The couple moved to Connecticut, where they had seven children; in 1792, Tallmadge was appointed postmaster for the town of Litchfield. He would later serve sixteen years in the House of Representatives (1801–17). Interestingly, in January 1817, one of the final matters Tallmadge undertook as a congressman before leaving office was to campaign against granting a pension to the three men (John Paulding, Isaac Van Wart, and David Williams) who first captured John André. According to a popular weekly circular of the time, Tallmadge argued that the men were hardly heroes, despite their public image, but

were, in fact, "of that class of people who passed between both armies, as often in one camp as in the
other." His objection was rooted in the fact that "when
Major André's boots were taken off by them, it was to
search for plunder, and not to detect treason. . . . If André could have given to these men the amount they demanded for his release, he never would have been hung
for a spy, nor in captivity." Tallmadge died on March 7,
1835. He was eighty-one years old.

Robert Townsend never spoke of his service, never
applied for a pension, never corrected those who assumed he had done nothing but tend his shop during
the war, and never, it seems, recovered emotionally
from the blow of Agent 355's capture and imprisonment. After the war he grew even more reserved and
reclusive. Dr. Peter Townsend, the son of his brother
Solomon, took a particular interest in his somber, silent
uncle Robert and often asked him about his service
during the war, but the older man was tight-lipped and
shared very little. Townsend kept to himself, staying
near his brothers and their families but never marrying
himself, though he may have fathered a child with his
French-Canadian housekeeper in the years following
the war. The child—a large, blond, blue-eyed boy who
resembled all the Townsend men except the slender,
dark Robert—was named Robert Townsend Jr. by his
mother, Mary. There was some suspicion that another
Townsend brother, the flirtatious William, the "flower
of the family," who happened at that time to share a
house with Robert, was actually the father. But Robert,
having no other children, took responsibility for the

boy's education and welfare; his will includes bequests for his supposed son, several nephews, and a niece. Townsend developed strong abolitionist beliefs and staunchly opposed any type of slave ownership; later in life he worked on behalf of some former slaves of his father's to help them gain their freedom. The man once known as Culper Junior died exactly three years after Benjamin Tallmadge, on March 7, 1838, at the age of eighty-four.

Abraham Woodhull married Mary Smith in 1781. He spent the rest of his life in Setauket, where he raised three children and served in roles of authority in the Suffolk County government. He never spoke much about his role in the spy ring. Mary died before Abraham; Lydia Terry became his second wife in his final years. He passed away on January 23, 1826, and was buried in the Setauket Presbyterian Church graveyard. In 1936, the Mayflower Chapter of the Daughters of the American Revolution erected the following marker near his simple headstone:

> *Friend and confidant of George Washington, Head of the Long Island Secret Service During the American Revolution he operated under the alias Samuel Culper, Sr. To him and his associates have been credited a large share of the success of the Army of the Revolution. Born in Setauket Oct. 7, 1750 in the original Woodhull homestead, son of Richard W. & Margaret Smith. Fifth generation from Richard Woodhull, the original grantee of a large portion of Brookhaven*

Town. He was a Presbyterian, occupying a "Pew of Authority" in the old church and doing much toward the building of the new church. He was a man of integrity punctual and precise in his business relations. He freed his slaves long before they were legally free. He filled numerous important positions being Magistrate in Setauket many years, Judge of the Court of Common Pleas 1793–1799, First Judge of Suffolk Co. from 1799–1810.

Agent 355, whose name and whose fate have both been lost to time, might have escaped imprisonment and gone on to live a long and happy life. Or she might have passed away somewhere in the dark, disease-infested hull of HMS *Jersey*. When the British left New York in November 1783, they abandoned the *Jersey* in the harbor, with several thousand starving prisoners still on board.

It is extremely difficult to learn much at all about the lives and deaths of those unlucky enough to have been captured. After the surrender of the British, the former colonists sought to piece together their shattered lives and homes; many records were lost, destroyed, or simply filed away without any thought to their deeper significance. Thousands of individuals were missing from battlefields, prison camps, and prison ships; thousands more were untraceable due to emigration, desertion, or simply westward movement into the newly opened territories beyond the Appalachians. In the mid-nineteenth century, as the generation who lived during the

Revolution was passing away, historians made some efforts to reconstruct lists of inmates' names by interviewing survivors of the *Jersey*. Though quite rare (and, since they were recalled several decades after the fact, not wholly reliable accounts), women's names do appear on some of these lists; none have yet been proved to be that of Agent 355.

For generations, the only Revolutionary War spy immortalized in history books was the brave but ultimately unsuccessful Nathan Hale. Tales of the Culper Ring were relegated to local legend or mystery (who was Culper Junior?). Learning the true identity of Washington's most consistent and valuable spy in the one city the general valued most was a pursuit undertaken by several prominent researchers, who analyzed the oral traditions and followed up on hunches. Townsend was always among those considered likely contenders, but the spy could not be unmasked until the "wagon full" of his letters was found in 1929 and given over to the care of Morton Pennypacker, who compared the writing with that of surviving Culper letters. At last a much more complete story of the ring could be told.

This momentous discovery was made during a dark and uncertain time in American history. The Great Depression threatened the very fabric of the nation, then all eyes were focused on the upheaval in Europe and the creeping threat in the Pacific. The United States was poised at the brink of its next great chapter and was not concerned with rewriting history. Despite Pennypacker's efforts to shine a light on these provincial heroes of Long Island, Manhattan, and coastal Connecticut, the Culpers once again sank into obscurity. But even if their story was not known across the nation, the fruits of their labors, their letters, and their lives were—and continue to be—felt from sea to shining sea in the freedoms and independence all American citizens enjoy.

Epilogue

We knew the story of the Culper Ring was important. We knew it was a story whose characters and events should be standard fare in history classes across the country. But what we didn't know was how relevant it still proves today within the intelligence community of the United States.

In February 2012, we were granted access to CIA Headquarters in Langley, Virginia, where we met with the agency's chief historian.

Outside the building is a statue honoring Nathan Hale's courage and patriotism; inside the building are exhibits on various spying operations of the past. But nowhere did we find homage to the Culper Ring—until we sat down for our meeting.

We were stunned to learn that the history of the ring is taught as part of the introductory training for new agents. Whether suggested by Washington or Tallmadge, or simply figured out, through bravery and intelligence, on their own, the methods used by these citizen-spies—the dead drops, the well-crafted back-stories, the compartmentalizing of intelligence, the secret encrypted code—are many of the same methods still used today by secret agents the world over.

And like the courageous men and women of our modern covert services, the Culpers worked in profound secrecy. They never sought credit, never received accolades, and never revealed the risks they took or the sacrifices they made to serve our country. Under the unblinking leadership of Benjamin Tallmadge, Washington's secret six served a newborn nation against a military that was considered to be unbeatable. The observation of Major George Beckwith bears repeating: "Washington did not really outfight the British, he simply outspied us!"

In this book, we have included photographs of some of the places, portraits, and humble graves that bear silent testimony to our nation's first and most accomplished ring of clandestine operatives.

There are no statues of these brave souls, whose feats should earn them a place of honor alongside the heroes of the Revolution. It is our sincerest hope that Robert Townsend, Abraham Woodhull, Caleb Brewster, Austin Roe, James Rivington, and Agent 355 will be given their rightful place in American history. Their extraordinary heroism and patriotism, unknown to their contemporaries, should not be forgotten. George Washington wouldn't have wanted it any other way—after all, he preserved their letters among his belongings, and it is because of him that we know their story.

Who Was Agent 355?

The greatest mystery surrounding the Culper Ring is the identity of Agent 355, the "lady who would outwit them all." Woodhull wrote of her but left no hints to her name. Robert Townsend deeply mourned her capture, closing his store for several weeks and falling into a deep depression, but he maintained secrecy even in his sorrow. No matter the pressure, the Culper Ring's protection of the sixth spy's name was watertight.

Since *George Washington's Secret Six* was first published in November 2013, we have received dozens of letters proposing theories of 355's identity. Readers told us of family lore connecting their relatives to 355. Some historians proposed names of women they believed may have been 355, while others argued that 355 was a composite of several women. Still others insisted that there was no 355 at all—that the line in Woodhull's letter was just a passing reference to a woman who had useful information but was not formally connected to the ring.

Inspired by readers' enthusiasm and by our own conviction that Agent 355 should not go unrecognized, we decided to dig deeper into our leads. After several false starts, we found seven women whose stories line up at least partially with our understanding of 355's story. Each of the seven candidates has evidence in her favor: she had proximity to known members of the Culper Ring, she had access to British information, she was known to have participated in espionage, or there is written or oral tradition testifying to her involvement. Yet each also has arguments against her: she wasn't present in New York for the entire war, her connections to the ring are tenuous or circumstantial at best, or her loyalties are questionable. Until further clues come to light, the mystery will remain, but in the meantime we present the seven most promising women our research has uncovered and leave it up to the readers to make up their own minds.

ANNA SMITH STRONG

The most enduring name in the running is Anna Smith Strong, a candidate whom we initially dismissed. However, several local legends tie her to the Culper Ring, so we decided to give her a closer look.

Anna was the daughter of New York's Chief Justice of the Supreme Court, and she was the wife of Selah Strong, a Patriot judge from Long Island who was imprisoned by the British in 1778. While some traditions state that Selah was held aboard one of New York's infamous prison ships, an article in Rivington's *Gazette* indicates that Strong was actually held in one of the "sugar house" prisons established by the British in Manhattan's sugar warehouses. Either way, he easily could have been known to members of the Culper Ring.

A tremendously resourceful and determined woman, Anna brought her husband's plight to the attention of her friends and family, hoping someone might be able to help secure his freedom. Ultimately, her resilience paid off, and Judge Strong was released and allowed to travel to American-controlled Connecticut. Meanwhile, Anna remained on Long Island, maintaining the family's estate so that the British troops could not declare it abandoned and confiscate it, which would have left her family destitute.

Eventually, enemy soldiers commandeered the Strong's home, but Anna and her children were permitted to reside in a small cottage on their land where they remained until the British left Long Island and the home was restored to them. Selah, too, was able to return to his wife and children following the cessation of hostilities.

The oral traditions linking Anna to the Culper Ring are at least a century old and revolve around rumors that she used the sheets on her clothesline to signal to Caleb Brewster in which cove he could safely land his whaleboat. The elevation and position of the Strongs' home make the story seem likely, as it offered a clear view of Long Island Sound. From there, anyone could easily track the movement of British patrol boats—exactly what the Culpers would have wanted to do.

Anna's bravery and dogged determination in the face of British oppression demonstrate she had the mettle for espionage. She also had a strong motive to bring about the defeat of the army that had torn apart her family. Add to that her location on Long Island, and she fits Agent 355's profile well.

Motive and location aside, however, there are several arguments against Anna's role as 355. First, the Strong family was determined to keep its land and property safe from the Crown's claims, which is why Anna and her children remained on Long Island rather than joining Selah in his exile in Connecticut. Anna probably would have avoided doing anything to threaten her already-tenuous legal status in British-occupied New York, as being caught spying (at best) would have landed her in prison and (at worst) would have seen her executed. Either way, her arrest would have left her children parentless, unless Selah could have convinced British authorities to safely transport them to American-controlled territory, and the family's possessions would have been lost because they no longer retained a foothold on the land.

For similar reasons, Anna probably would have avoided the social scene (and thus the potential gossip) of New York or any other town outside her immediate area. Had she ventured far from home, the British could have seized her land and brought all her efforts to naught. Thus, her pool of information would have been limited to the region that Woodhull, Roe, and Brewster already covered for the Culpers.

Finally, since her husband was already a known dissident working actively against the British, the Strong family was under close observation by the

Crown. If she knew that she was being watched, it is unlikely (though, admittedly, not impossible) that she would have risked drawing attention to herself by changing where or how she hung her laundry or carried out any other household tasks. It is possible that she was brave (or foolish) enough to ignore these dangers and spy against the British, but such recklessness would have been surprising for the Culpers.

SALLY TOWNSEND

Another woman linked to the Culper Ring through popular oral tradition is Sally Townsend, the younger sister of Robert and the object of Colonel Simcoe's affections during his stay at Raynham Hall.

Born in 1760, Sally was eighteen when the Queen's Rangers took up residence in her family's Oyster Bay home in 1778. With their older brothers settled in homes of their own, only the Townsend daughters, Sally and Phebe, were left behind to help their parents serve the soldiers who had invited themselves to set up headquarters under the family's roof. Both girls quickly became favorites among the young men, with Sally capturing the attention and the heart of the Colonel, who wrote a lengthy, thirteen-stanza poem in her honor, beginning:

> *Fairest Maid, where all is fair*
> *Beauty's pride and Nature's care;*
> *To you my heart I must resign*
> *O choose me for your Valentine!*

Given Simcoe's affection for her and her proximity to the British troops in her home, Sally would have had every chance to learn British plans. There is a tradition, in fact, that Sally was about to serve the troops a plate of doughnuts when she overhead Simcoe discussing the plans to take over West Point thanks to Benedict Arnold's treachery. The story has it that she rushed to get word to her brother in Manhattan immediately so that he could alert Tallmadge and General Washington.

Unfortunately, it is unlikely that the incident with the doughnuts ever took place, since the tale does not seem to have come into existence until more than a century after the alleged events. The timeline is also off; the Rangers left the Townsend home in the spring of 1779, and the betrayal at West Point did not occur until September of the following year—and there is no record that Simcoe ever made an effort to correspond with Sally after his troops left Raynham Hall.

Further, while her father and brothers were Patriots, there is no reason to believe that Sally objected to the presence of British soldiers in the house. Instead, it seems that both she and Phebe enjoyed the situation, and Sally may have returned Simcoe's affection. She kept Simcoe's valentine until the day she died, and there is a window etching made by one of the soldiers in the original glass of the house that reads, "To the adorable Miss Sally Sarah Townsend." Simcoe and his Rangers left Raynham Hall after their six-month stay, and Sally, who never married, died in 1842, at the age of 82. If she did love the British officer, it's doubtful she would have worked against him.

MARY UNDERHILL

Mary Woodhull Underhill, the older sister of Abraham Woodhull, is another Culper sister linked to the ring. Married shortly before the war started, she and her husband moved to New York City to operate a boarding house on Queen Street in downtown Manhattan, which they maintained during the course of the war.

As Abraham Woodhull's sister, Mary could easily have held the trust of the ring. Her brother often stayed at the Underhills' boarding house, as did Austin Roe and Caleb Brewster on occasion, so Mary would have known the Culpers well and would have had opportunities to pass on information. Her husband, Amos, is said to have functioned as a satellite member of the ring—most likely acting as a courier—so Mary's involvement with the ring seems even more plausible.

However, the case against Mary is threefold. First, an emotional objection: Abraham Woodhull's letters often mentioned his fear of being caught, and it is hard to picture a man so anxious about his own spying recruiting his family to join him in such a dangerous task. Involving Mary would have increased the possibility of suspicion falling upon the family—especially following the severe beating that Colonel Simcoe inflicted upon Abraham and Mary's father, Richard Woodhull, in the spring of 1779. Then again, if Amos was already a spy, this objection is weak.

Second, there is a practical objection. The Underhills made their living by running a boarding house that would have provided temporary shelter for travelers or visitors to the city, not to soldiers who were stationed there. While it may have seemed a prime location to hear gossip and rumors, the boarding house was probably not frequented by soldiers or locals who were the more likely sources of useful information about the goings-on in the city.

Finally, while there are indications that Amos may have been involved with some minor operations during the early months of the ring's existence, there is no indication that Woodhull nor Townsend ever fully initiated Amos or Mary into the ring (after all, Amos doesn't have a covert name or numeric assignment in the code). And if Mary Woodhull Underhill was indeed Agent 355, why would it have been Townsend rather than Woodhull who would have been the most distraught following what seems to have been her capture after the Arnold affair was unmasked? Mary could have been 355, but there are too many questions about her involvement to know for sure.

BETTY FLOYD

Robert Townsend's distant cousin Elizabeth Floyd was born in August 1758 on Long Island. Little is known of her other than that she was a niece of William Floyd, a signer of the Declaration of Independence, but her familial ties to Townsend coupled with the possibility that she may have died aboard a British prison ship brought her name to our attention.

Though the official record books for the British

prison ship HMS *Jersey* have been lost, in 1888 the Brooklyn Historical Society compiled a list of prisoners based upon prisoners' diaries, family lore, and some loosely kept records from the British War Department. Of the eight thousand names listed, only about two dozen belong to women or are androgynous, and a "Betty Floyd" appeared among them. She was listed as having died aboard the prison ship, making her a likely match for Agent 355. (The other names have proven untraceable or are connected with women who appear to be wholly unaffiliated with the Culpers.)

Unfortunately, the case for Betty is inconclusive. First, it is possible that the "Betty" listed in the prison ship records is an error. Some versions of the *Jersey* prisoner list have only a "Barry" or "Berry" Floyd, and no "Betty" or any other derivatives of "Elizabeth" paired with the same last name. And since the lists were compiled more than a century after the events occurred, their reliability as historical documents is questionable.

Even if a Betty Floyd did die on the *Jersey*, we cannot conclusively link her to the Culpers. "Elizabeth Floyd" was a quite common name at the time, and there were several women with that name living on Long Island and in New York City during the revolution, making a positive identification of the right Betty difficult. Further, the most likely Elizabeth Floyd we could find (the one who came from a Patriot family and had family connections to Robert Townsend) died in 1820 at the age of 62, which means that she could not be the same woman who died aboard a British prison ship in New York Harbor.

We can't find records of a woman named Elizabeth or Betty Floyd living in New York City or on Long Island who died at the time when the *Jersey* was being used as a prison ship. It's possible that an unknown and undocumented Betty was indeed 355 and died on the ship, but if that is the case, her story is lost to time.

PEGGY SHIPPEN ARNOLD

One surprising name as a possible Agent 355 is Peggy Shippen Arnold, Benedict Arnold's second wife. Despite her marriage to the traitor, she was a socialite with strong Loyalist connections and a close relationship with John André. Considering her friendship with British officers, the deep secrecy surrounding her identity as 355 would be understandable.

Though Peggy came from a Loyalist family, her father, Edward Shippen IV, held moderate views and occasionally took the Patriots' side in the years leading up to the Revolution. On September 10, 1765, in the midst of the Stamp Act controversy, Edward wrote to his father in England: "I think the Act an oppressive one, and I wish a Scheme for Repeal of it could be fallen on[.]" Five weeks later, on October 17, he wrote about the recent arrival of a baby boy, noting: "On the 9th Inst. Peggy [Edward's wife and Peggy's mother] presented me with a son, born just in time enough to breath [sic] about three weeks the Air of Freedom; for after the first of November we may call ourselves the Slaves of England."

Edward's moderate views seem to have persisted at

least through the years just before the outbreak of war. George Washington was even a dinner guest at the Shippen family table in late September 1774 during the First Continental Congress in Philadelphia. The future Mrs. Arnold, who was fifteen at the time, later wrote that "nobody in America could revere his character more than I did." In the end, however, having been educated in Britain and retaining strong ties to his family there, Edward remained true to King George and fixed himself as a solid Loyalist.

Peggy's early inclinations to the American cause might seem negated by her later stance, but there is more to the story, according to her family. From the mid-nineteenth through the early twentieth century, the Shippen family argued that Peggy was innocent of treason, claiming Washington was impressed by her hysterical response to the news of her husband's treachery and had believed in her innocence. As evidence, they pointed out that Washington made special provisions for Peggy's safe passage back to her father's home, an unlikely course of action if he considered her a traitor.

The family also argued that Aaron Burr, whose memoirs are the main source for the stories of Peggy's actions following the discovery of her husband's treason, was a tainted witness. A rather dubious figure in American history, Burr is famous for having killed Secretary of the Treasury Alexander Hamilton in an ill-fated duel and was a famed ladies' man. The Shippens argued that Peggy had scorned his advances when he escorted her to the family's home in Philadelphia following Arnold's defection and that Burr made the accusations as retribution.

If this revisionist account is true and it clears Peggy's name, her position with the British army supports arguments that she was an American spy. The letters and parcels she conveyed between British soldiers and their sweethearts could have been cover for her spying activities with the Culpers. She was known and respected by André and could have learned of his movements and intentions. Her marriage to a respected (if unpopular) senior officer in the Continental Army would have given the Culpers and even General Washington himself every reason to trust her. Her social position, acquaintances, and allegiances through marriage gave her the perfect cover to convey sensitive information to Tallmadge and, from him, to Washington.

We'd love nothing more than to reveal that the wife of Benedict Arnold secretly worked against his schemes, but the evidence against Peggy still seems insurmountable. A number of letters between Benedict Arnold, John André, and General Henry Clinton indicate that the planned betrayal was well known to all the players, including Peggy. And letters between Benedict and Peggy indicate that Peggy was the more powerful member of the couple; Arnold would have done just about anything to please her. If Peggy was truly a Patriot, it is highly unlikely that Arnold—who always seemed to fear that she would leave him for someone younger, more powerful, or richer—would have switched sides and risked alienating her.

The Shippen family's accusations of Burr came years after Peggy's death, and there is no other evidence that Burr made any kind of a "pass" at Peggy or that he lied about her behavior and confession. In fact, Burr was loyal to the Shippen family, having stayed with Peggy's parents for a few months during his childhood after the death of his own parents, and he always spoke of their kind treatment of him in grateful and glowing terms. Unless new information comes to light, Peggy's name remains tainted, and her role as 355 seems highly unlikely.

SARAH HORTON TOWNSEND

One of the most intriguing possible identities of Agent 355 is Sarah Horton Townsend, the wife of Robert Townsend's cousin Samuel. Records indicate that Samuel and Sarah lived in Norwich, NY, but it is unclear whether those records refer to the Norwich in Chenango County, some 215 miles from Oyster Bay, or the village of East Norwich, a mere four miles south of Oyster Bay. If it is the latter, which seems more likely because of their family ties, Samuel and Sarah would have been perfectly situated to help the Culpers.

During the war, Samuel served as a captain in the Continental Army. He was taken captive by the British during the late spring or summer of 1782 and held in Provost Prison, on the site of what is now City Hall Park in downtown Manhattan. By that time, the couple had a daughter named Sarah (born in December

1779), and in early August 1782 Samuel wrote to his wife with longing for his young family even as he voiced frustration at the delays in securing his release:

> *Hope my friends in the country have not forgot me. I would not wish to entertain a thought but they will use their endeavors to procure my exchange, but must confess I am at a loss for the reason that that has not been done before this time. I have repeatedly been informed that there are a number of prisoners at West Point, Peekskill, and Poughkeepsie, for whom, possibly, I could have been exchanged before this time, if properly attended to. My best respects to all friends . . . and beg that they would, without delay, apply in my behalf to their Excellencies General Washington and Governor Clinton, which I have no doubt will have the desired effect. However, as the fortune of war brought me here, I hope you will make yourself as easy as possible under present difficulties, as I am determined patiently to wait the wished-for day when I may enjoy the happiness of being present with my family.*

Though Samuel's capture and imprisonment is about a year and a half too late to be one of the arrests following the Culpers's unmasking of Arnold, his release raises the possibility of a different connection to the ring. Not only did George Washington orchestrate Townsend's release, but also a letter written by

Townsend to his wife was preserved among Washington's papers at his headquarters in Newburgh, New York. Washington's attention to Townsend's case indicates that Sarah had an avenue directly to the commander-in-chief's ear. If she was indeed spying for Washington, Tallmadge might have been willing to bring her petition on her husband's behalf before Washington, who would have owed debt of gratitude for her work and intervened accordingly.

Sarah has proximity, a connection to the Culpers, and a service from Washington in her favor, but there is one factor that weighs against her: She would have been five months pregnant in mid-August of 1779 when Woodhull made mention of the enigmatic "lady." Five months into their pregnancies, many middle-and upper-class women in the eighteenth century were preparing to enter into what was commonly referred to as their "confinement"—a period before they gave birth when they would not attend any social gatherings nor be seen in public at all, if it could be avoided. Sarah's pregnancy probably would have removed her from most sources of sensitive information, making it difficult for her to help the Culpers. She may have found a way to glean information from other women, but the danger of doing so makes her role as a spy seem unlikely.

ELIZABETH BURGIN

The woman with the most compelling story is Elizabeth Burgin (or "Bergin" in some records). A widow with three young children in British-occupied New York, she devoted much of her time ministering to the needs of the American prisoners languishing in the squalor of the prison ships in New York Harbor. Most of the prisoners' food, blankets, clothing, or medicine had to be privately supplied by family members, religious figures, or benevolent patrons, and Burgin helped to provide these supplies. But that is not all she did.

Unbeknownst to the British, Burgin worked with a man named George Higday to help smuggle prisoners off the ships to freedom. No one knows exactly how the escapes were planned and carried out, and since the prison hulks were generally treated as floating rubbish bins where people were forgotten, there was no systematic record keeping to alert the British to the dwindling number of prisoners. All told, Higday and Burgin succeeded in smuggling more than two hundred American prisoners to safety before their activities were discovered.

In a letter dated June 27, 1779, George Washington wrote to Benjamin Tallmadge about the possibility of incorporating George Higday into the Culper Ring. Unfortunately, this letter, which mentioned Higday by name and was written in regular (rather than invisible) ink, was captured along with Tallmadge's horse by the British on July 2. Higday's house was raided on July 13 and his wife (probably in the hopes of obtaining a lighter sentence for her husband) offered up the name "Elizabeth Burgin" as a possible spy and confirmed prisoner smuggler. When the British followed up on the tip and found that a large number of Americans were missing from the prison hulks, they set out to bring Elizabeth in for questioning on July 17—but she was nowhere to be found. Major General James Pattinson announced a £200 reward for her capture, but by then she had managed to flee from Manhattan to Long Island.

It is not known where she stayed on Long Island, but she remained in hiding there for four to six weeks with some trusted and sympathetic friends who were familiar with the work she and Higday had accomplished. By early September she had made her way across the sound to Connecticut in a whaleboat piloted by a man named William Sherridon, who followed a route that Caleb Brewster had used. "I made my escape with him, we being chased by two boats halfway to the Sound, then got to New England," she later wrote.

From Connecticut, she made her way to newly-liberated Philadelphia and began two petitions. The first was to the British to allow her re-admittance to New York to retrieve her children, who had been presumably left in the care of friends as she fled. This was swiftly granted, and in late September or early October she traveled under a flag of truce to New York City to pick up her children, and the reunited family then traveled back to Philadelphia together. They were forced to abandon all their property and belongings, which meant that the Burgins arrived in Philadelphia nearly destitute—but with their lives.

It was then that Elizabeth Burgin launched her other petition: She appealed to lawmakers for a pension to help support her family, as she was not eligible for either a soldier's pension (as she had never served) or the war widows' pension. On November 19, 1779, she wrote to the commander-in-chief directly, outlining both her service to the country and her family's need. Five weeks later, on Christmas Day, Washington gave orders to the ration master in Philadelphia that Elizabeth and her children should be allowed to draw upon the stores for supplies, which greatly relieved the family's distress but still left her a refugee with a bounty on her head and with three children to support in a time and place that did not look kindly on women working outside the home.

In July 1781, she wrote another letter explaining that she was encountering difficulties in receiving the rations for which Washington had approved her. She asked for a job as a seamstress for the Continental Army to help support herself and her children; instead, the following month, Congress approved a measure that would grant her a pension for life in the total of $53.30 per year. She was one of a very small number of women granted a pension from the government, and records indicate that she continued to receive the annuity through at least 1787, though nothing is known of her life or death beyond that point.

The evidence in favor of Burgin as Agent 355 is, as with all other contenders, circumstantial, at best. However, several facts make a compelling case for her being 355.

First and foremost, there is a clear connection between Burgin and Higday, and between Higday and the Culpers. Additionally, Burgin's work liberating more than two hundred prisoners establishes her identity as a risk-taker and wildly successful covert agent; surely a little spying work would be a small danger after what she had already accomplished.

Also of significance is the timeline of events. Burgin fled Manhattan on or around July 17, 1779, and stayed on Long Island for at least a month. The letter in which Woodhull writes about 355 in such glowing terms, bragging that she will "outwit them all" is dated August 15, 1779—during the period in which Burgin was known to be hiding on Long Island and possibly making the acquaintance of members of the Culper Ring.

Finally, it is important to note that the news regarding the stolen currency plates and paper in Philadelphia that were intended to be used in a forgery ring in New York (as recounted in chapter 9) came out in late November of 1779—not long after Burgin and her family were settled in Philadelphia. Perhaps it was she who first caught wind of the story of the theft and alerted the Culpers to be on the lookout for any news that might indicate the intended destination and plans for the stolen goods.

There are some obstacles to establishing Burgin's identity as the female member of the Culper Ring, however. There is no evidence that Burgin ever returned to New York after she retrieved her children in the fall of 1779, and any information regarding the situation in Manhattan and the troops stationed there (especially John André) in 1780 would almost certainly have come from a resident of the city rather than someone living elsewhere. This absence of evidence does not prove that she was not in New York or did not have some other means of accessing sensitive information, but it makes her case inconclusive.

THE MYSTERY PERSISTS

It is a testimony to the effectiveness of the Culpers as covert agents that so few clues exist as to Agent 355's identity. Each candidate we have found fits one or two parts of the puzzle (e.g., a relationship with André or with one of the Culpers; a proven history of covert activity) but falls short in another aspect (e.g., she is not known to have been in New York at the right times; she would not have had the social connections required to gain the information). Further, there is no evidence that any of our possible candidates, besides the enigmatic Betty Floyd, were ever captured by the British.

Who was Agent 355? There are several possible conclusions. We may be missing information about one of the women profiled that would prove she was 355. Another woman, completely unknown at this point, may have been the spy. Or, 355 may not have existed as an individual—several women may have operated under the code name. The one conclusion that is *not* possible is that 355 does not matter. Even if she did not exist as one person, several women risked their lives to serve, and one unknown friend of the ring *was* imprisoned following the unmasking of Arnold's treachery. That heroism deserves to be honored.

We care about 355's story not only because we enjoy a good mystery but also because we still believe she was a real, living and breathing woman who sacrificed her safety—and maybe even her life—for the sake of our country. We want to learn not just who she was but what she did—and what happened to her as a result. Our research remains inconclusive, but we're hopeful that one day another Morton Pennypacker will find a new cache of letters revealing the identity of the six's most secret spy. Only when we know can we pay her the honor she deserves.

ACKNOWLEDGMENTS

There are so many great people responsible for the completion of this book. I urge you to read what follows and take note of them all. First, I must thank my longtime friend Bruce Stegner, whom I informed of this ring in 1988; he held on to the concept and has relentlessly researched the secret six ever since, unwavering in the belief that this story just had to be told to a larger audience. And thanks to our respective families—Renee, Rebecca, Olivia, and Julia Stegner; my wife, Dawn, Bryan, Kirstyn, and Kaitlyn Kilmeade; and Jeanette, Will, and Madeleine Yaeger—for indulging our excitement about the story and mirroring our enthusiasm as every aspect of the ring was brought to light and life.

Thanks to the brilliant Tiffany Yecke Brooks, without whom we could not have researched and written this project. Tiffany has worked with Don for years but absolutely fell into her sweet spot on this book, because it combined her passion for historical research with creative writing. She kept both of us on task.

Roger Ailes, who allows me to work at the most patriotic company in America, is due a tremendous amount of thanks. He underlined the need for all of us to know our history and recognize the incredible bravery and selflessness of the first generations of Americans, which are demonstrated in the story of the six brave individuals who made up America's first spy ring.

Of course, this book could not have been written without the guidance of all-star Fox VP Bill Shine, a Long Islander who is endlessly supportive and understands the significance of the story because it happened in his backyard. We also owe a salute to Diane Brandi, who was the first to hear the book pitch; without her guidance and support the project would never gotten done.

I must also salute my *Fox & Friends* cohosts, Steve Doocy, Gretchen Carlson, and Alisyn Camerota, who have heard me talk about this story for years and could not have been more supportive. Thanks for stepping up to help me during her free time go to Alyson Mansfield, executive producer of *Kilmeade & Friends*. I also can't say enough for the producing team on *Fox & Friends*, led by Lauren Petterson and Jennifer Rauchet, for their faith in the project before they read even a word on paper.

To Bob Barnett, who believed in the project so much that he wisely navigated us to the Sentinel imprint of the Penguin Group to see it through—thank you. We are in awe of his perpetually sunny, upbeat approach to life and humbled by his loyalty to us even as he handles the most famous and powerful people in the world.

Don and I were truly thrilled and moved to know that Adrian Zackheim, president and publisher of Sentinel, would be editing the book, and it flowered under his skilled eye. And what can we say about Bria Sandford that would be sufficient thanks for her role, except that she is a true professional in every way, thrives on making deadlines happen, is endlessly patient, and is extremely bright? To say that she was kind of important to this project would be like saying that LeBron James is kind of important to the Miami Heat.

Over the twenty-plus years that I have spent learning about this story, many passionate people and organizations have shared with me their hard-earned knowledge and research of the ring and these historical figures. I fear I might leave someone out, but here it goes nonetheless.

Steve Russell Boerner of the East Hampton Library Long Island Collection offered patience and insight that were critical in so many ways to the success of the book. Gina Piastuck and Frank Sorrentino from the collection brought Morton Pennypacker back to life, and thanks to Frank's rapid translation of the Woodhull-Townsend logs, we were able to break much new ground on this story. Thanks to Andrea Meyer and John Burke for thier work on Agent 355. And the good people at Black Rock history in Connecticut were a great resource for our Caleb Brewster research.

The invaluable John Tsunis not only gave us a conference room at his Holiday Inn to hold a major secret six summit with historians from around Long Island but also introduced me to Gloria Rocchio and the

Ward Melville Heritage Organization. Gloria shed light on many aspects of this story and has been a stalwart in supporting the legacy of the ring and preserving Long Island history. She has been not only a great help but also a great friend. Michael Colucci and Deborah Boudreau, also part of the Ward Melville group, were a tremendous source of assistance and encouragement.

We could not have seen this project through without the cooperation and help of the people of the Raynham Hall Museum in Oyster Bay. Claire Bellerjeau, Townsend family historian, is one of the most knowledgeable people you will meet on the era and the ring; her knowledge and enthusiasm were essential in making Robert Townsend and the rest of his family come alive on these pages. Collections manager Nicole Menchise and executive director Harriet Gerard Clark could not have been more helpful or insightful. They allowed us to walk the house as Robert Townsend did centuries ago, fueling our motivation to spread this story to millions more.

I could not imagine carrying out this project without Barbara Russell, town of Brookhaven historian. She not only educated me about the Setauket spies of 1780 but also brought me to the locations as they stand today. Elizabeth Kahn Kaplan helped me not only with the story but also, as curator of the Three Village Historical Society's exhibit, got my family excited with her tremendous knowledge and passion. If you truly want to understand how special this revolutionary spy story is, just spend a few minutes with Bev

Tyler. He has an awe-inspiring depth of knowledge on the topic and played a key role in acquiring many of the sketches and maps you see in the book.

Special thanks are due, too, to Matt Arthur, Living History Program coordinator at Tryon Palace Historic Sites and Gardens in New Bern, North Carolina, and to Rebecca Reimer Arthur, lecturer in history at Liberty University, for sharing their tremendous knowledge of the era and genealogical investigations during the early stages of writing this book.

If there was one trip that galvanized our belief that this was a book that should be written, it was the journey we took to CIA Headquarters in Langley, Virginia. When we heard the CIA's historians and agents talk so movingly about the success of this ring and its methods, we knew that our interest and awe were justified. At their request I will not list their names, but I would like to acknowledge the CIA Office of Public Affairs and the CIA's historical staff.

Finally, I'd like to thank the CIA Officers Memorial Foundation (www.ciamemorialfoundation.org), the Armed Forces Foundation (www.armedforces foundation.org), and the Wounded Warrior Project (www.woundedwarriorproject.org) for their support for today's generation of fighters and spies, which needs support more than ever before.

SELECTED SOURCES

Allen, Thomas B., and Cheryl Harness. *George Washington, Spymaster: How America Outspied the British and Won the Revolutionary War.* Washington, D.C.: National Geographic, 2004.

A highly accessible book, this is a great starting point for adults and older children alike who are interested in the spying activities under Washington's command during the Revolution. It is the result of solid research and offers a good overview of espionage activities throughout the war.

Bakeless, John Edwin. *Turncoats, Traitors, and Heroes.* New York: Da Capo, 1998.

This work provides a look at the unfortunate incident of Nathan Hale, the saga of Benedict Arnold's treachery, and many other covert operations in the American theater during the war, including the incredible adventure of John Champe and his attempt to kidnap Arnold back for the Patriots.

Baker, William S. "Itinerary of General Washington from June 15, 1775, to December 23, 1783." *The Pennsylvania Magazine of History and Biography* 15, no. 1 (1891): 41–87. http://jstor.org.

Crary, Catherine Snell. "The Tory and the Spy: The Double Life of James Rivington," *The William and Mary Quarterly*, 3rd ser., 16, no. 1 (January 1959): 61–72. Accessed online March 22, 2013.

> This article pulls together a number of primary sources that shed light on Rivington's spying activities, including his contribution to the victory at Yorktown, that were previously discounted as apocryphal, and therefore unreliable, by many historians.

Fernow, Brian, ed. *Documents Relating to the Colonial History of the State of New York.* Vol. 15. *State Archives,* vol. 1. Albany, NY: Weed, Parsons and Company, 1887.

"George Washington and the Culper Spy Ring." Stony Brook University Libraries. http://guides.library.stonybrook.edu/culper-spy-ring.

Kerber, Linda K. *Women of the Republic: Intellect and Ideology in Revolutionary America.* Chapel Hill: University of North Carolina Press, 1997.

Macy, Harry, Jr. "Robert Townsend, Jr., of New York City." *The New York Genealogical and Biographical Record* 126 (1995): 25–34, 108–12, 192–98.

Perhaps more than any other single source, this article shed light on the physical appearance and relationships of the Townsend family and also offered an in-depth look at Robert Townsend and his interaction with the child named Robert Townsend Jr. after the war.

Nagy, John A. *Invisible Ink: Spycraft of the American Revolution*. Yardley, PA: Westholme, 2010.

Nagy has compiled a searching and fascinating examination of various techniques used by spies throughout the American colonies and abroad to communicate covertly. His exploration of the history of invisible ink prior to the Culper stain's development by Sir James Jay, as well as the use of that particular formula, was tremendously helpful for this book.

——. *Spies in the Continental Capital: Espionage Across Pennsylvania During the American Revolution*. Yardley, PA: Westholme, 2011.

New York Gazette & Weekly. Templeton & Stewart. April 25, 1774. Mercury issue 1174, p. 2.

——. Templeton & Stewart. August 15, 1774. Mercury issue 1192, p. 4.

——. Templeton & Stewart. February 27, 1775. Mercury issue 1220, p. 3.

Norton, Mary Beth. *Liberty's Daughters: The Revolutionary Experience of American Women, 1750–1800.* Ithaca, NY: Cornell University Press, 1996.

A fascinating compilation of primary sources, this book offers valuable insight into the challenges and perils of women living in war-torn areas during the Revolution, including the lighthearted letter from Lord Rawdon about the outbreak of sexual assaults against ladies in British-occupied Staten Island.

Paul, Joel Richard. *Unlikely Allies: How a Merchant, a Playwright, and a Spy Saved the American Revolution.* New York: Riverhead, 2009.

A detailed account of the covert activities of the French government via the fabricated Roderigue Hortalez & Company, Paul's research offers a dynamic and intriguing reconstruction of the events leading up to, and resulting from, the smuggling efforts.

Pennypacker, Morton. *General Washington's Spies.* Walnut Creek, CA: Aegean Park, 1999.

Pennypacker's 1939 publication of the Culper letters includes a narrative of many of the events involving the ring, as they were known at the time, as well as both transcripts and photographs of many of the original letters exchanged between several of the ring's members, Tallmadge, and Washington. It was absolutely invaluable not only to the composition of this book but also to understanding the Culper story in general.

————. *Two Spies: Nathan Hale and Robert Town-send*. Boston and New York: Houghton Mifflin, 1930.

Pierce, Kara. "A Revolutionary Masquerade: The Chronicles of James Rivington." Binghamton University. n.d. http://www.binghamton.edu/history/resources/journal-of-history/chronicles-of-james-rivington.html.

> Pierce's article offers a fascinating look into the personal life of James Rivington as well as his spying activities during the war and was an important resource in helping to reconstruct Rivington's mysterious character.

Pierce, Susan M. *The History of Raynham Hall*. Thesis, Columbia University, 1986.

> This thesis study provided many helpful details about the architectural history of the Townsend family homestead and its position in colonial Oyster Bay.

Rose, Alexander. *Washington's Spies: The Story of America's First Spy Ring*. New York: Bantam, 2006.

> Rose undertook a tremendous depth of research to complete his book, and it served as an excellent starting point in quite a few places for our own investigation into the matter. Especially helpful was his engagement with disparate primary sources that together formed a fuller picture of the Culper Ring's activities and accomplishments.

Ross, Peter. "A Few Revolutionary Heroes—General Woodhull—Colonel Tallmadge—General Parsons—Colonel Meigs." *A History of Long Island, from Its Earliest Settlement to the Present Time*. New York and Chicago: Lewis, 1902.

Schecter, Barnet. *The Battle for New York: The City at the Heart of the American Revolution*. New York: Walker, 2002.

 This book proved especially important in helping us to understand the vital importance of New York City to the overall outcome of the war and allowed us to better grasp the significance of its political, strategic, and symbolic impact. It also helped us explain the high regard that Washington had for his spy network within the city.

Tallmadge, Benjamin. *Memoir of Colonel Benjamin Tallmadge Prepared by Himself at the Request of His Children*. New York: Thomas Holman, 1858. Reprint, New York: New York Times, 1968.

 Most of the accounts of Tallmadge's activities and emotions come directly from his own pen in the memoirs he originally wrote in the final years of his life and first published for widespread distribution in 1858. Rarely is an author so lucky as to have the impressions and reflections of a historical figure in his original words. This is an especially valuable resource for any student of the American Revolution or Washington's spycraft.

Townsend, Robert. "Account Book of Robert Townsend, Merchant, of Oyster Bay Township, N.Y., and New York, N.Y., Begun November 23, 1779, and Continued to March 29, 1781." Transcription. East Hampton Library, Long Island Collection, East Hampton, NY.

> The firsthand information revealed in this document was extremely helpful in understanding more about how Townsend operated first in Oyster Bay and later in Manhattan. Both the detailed entries and the periods of inactivity reveal a great deal about Townsend's patterns of behavior, possible emotional struggles, and business habits in managing his shop and his daily life.

Woodhull, Mary Gould, and Francis Bowes Stevens. *Woodhull Genealogy: The Woodhull Family in England and America*. Philadelphia: H. T. Coates, 1904.

INDEX